vegetables

JimHole LoisHole

questions & ANSWERS

volume 4

vegetables

Practical Advice and the
Science Behind It

H
HOLE'S
ENJOY GARDENING

Published by Hole's
101 Bellerose Drive
St. Albert, Alberta Canada
T8N 8N8

Printed in Canada   5   4   3   2   1

National Library of Canada Cataloguing in Publication Data

Hole, Jim, 1956-
  Vegetables

  (Questions and answers ; 4)
  Includes index.
  ISBN 0-9682791-8-X

  1. Vegetables—Miscellanea. 2. Vegetable gardening—Miscellanea. I. Hole, Lois, 1933- II. Title. III. Series: Questions & answers (St. Albert, Alta.) ; 4.
SB323.C3H65 2001   635   C00-911649-4

Colour separations and film by Elite Lithographers, Edmonton, Alberta, Canada
Printed and bound by Quality Color Press, Edmonton, Alberta, Canada
Illustrations by Donna McKinnon

Contents

Acknowledgements

Thanks to our staff members for collecting these questions, especially the staff in our new call centre, who often fielded hundreds of calls per day and yet still found the time to record the questions used for this book.

Thanks also to those people who sent questions via e-mail at yourquestions@enjoygardening.com. Keep them coming!

Finally, from the Hole family, our thanks go out to our neighbours, our extended family, and our market-garden customers, who helped us learn about vegetable gardening from the roots up. During those lean early years, you made all the difference.

The *Q&A* Series—
Practical Advice and the Science Behind It

It comes as no surprise that *Vegetables: Practical Advice and the Science Behind It* is, to date, the most information-packed entry in the Q&A series. While *Bedding Plants*, *Roses*, and *Perennials* covered many of the most common questions, there was still plenty of territory to explore in this book. Vegetables lie at the heart of gardening: they sustain us, challenge us, and reward us with their rich flavours and textures. Not many people need to garden to feed the family these days, yet thousands of gardeners continue to plant vegetables, a testament to their enduring value.

Success is built on a solid foundation of questions. Every innovation comes about because someone wondered, "How does this process work? And how can I make it work better?" A good question can open up whole new worlds—new ways of doing things, new perspectives, and new information about secrets once hidden.

That information is what good gardening is all about. Our goal has always been to provide gardeners, no matter what their skill level, with the information they need to grow beautiful plants—and to accomplish this in the most enjoyable manner. Accordingly, different people want different kinds of information. We've answered the questions in two parts: a short answer for those who are eager to solve a problem and get back to their projects, and a more in-depth answer for those who want to spend a little time learning what makes their favourite hobby tick. In short, we deliver practical advice and the science behind it.

At Hole's, we've always tried to ask the right questions, and to listen carefully when they come from someone else. The questions in the *Q&A* books didn't spring from our heads. They were collected from hundreds of people, from coast to coast. Over the past dozen years, we've been recording the best questions we've run across, from the simple questions we thought beginning gardeners could identify with to the head-scratchers that gave us pause. The inquiries came from walk-in customers, letters, phone calls, and e-mail messages. Some came from audiences during one or another of our radio or television appearances; others from the folks we've spoken to at gardening talks all across the continent. A few came from our own employees during the day-to-day operations of our greenhouse. No matter what the source, each inquiry contained within itself a valuable piece of information: it told us what people wanted to know, and gave us a guide with which to build this series of books.

Answering these questions has been as valuable for us as for the questioners. They've pushed us to the limits of our knowledge, urging us to dig deeper for the truth.

Lois Hole and Jim Hole
February 2001

Introduction

by Jim Hole

I grew up with a fascination for vegetables. The first time I bit into a freshly harvested cob of corn, I knew I had to unlock its secrets. Why did it taste so good? How did it grow? What did the leaves do? Why was there hairy stuff on the pointy end of the cob?

My curiosity drew me right into the fields of our St. Albert farm, alongside my folks and my brother, Bill. Working in the garden was a great opportunity to investigate its many mysteries.

A Promise of Plenty

When I was very young, I was fascinated by seed catalogues, chiefly because they were filled with pictures of delectable vegetables. Mom ordered numerous catalogues every year, from a variety of seed companies, and they usually arrived in early January. I was entranced by the enormous potential of just a few small packets of seed. To think that for a few cents, you could get enough seed to plant rows and rows of corn, or radishes, or lettuce. Whenever Mom placed an order, I was beset by anticipation. Spring always seemed too far away.

When the seeds finally arrived, they came in big five-pound bags, perfect for sticking your hands into just to feel the varied textures. And I loved the strong, distinctive smells, especially the dill, carrot, squash, and pumpkin seed. There wasn't much time to get lost in the sensual delights of seed, though: even before the snow had completely melted, we were out in the garden, mapping out which seeds would be planted where. "Cucumbers need plenty of heat; we'll plant them here on the south end," Mom or Dad would say. "We should rotate the carrots this year. The old cornfield won't do…last year's stalks are still there." And so it went, a day or two of carefully planning how the year's vegetable crop would take shape.

As soon as the ground was thawed, we were planting, no matter how early in the year it may have seemed. Our neighbours—Mrs. Sernowski in particular—had taught by example that when you gambled and planted early, you won far more often than you lost. To win the race against the onset of winter you've got to leap from the gate at full speed. It wasn't just a matter of impatience. Sure, we wanted an early harvest for our own dinner table, but when we started our market-gardening business, it was a matter of survival. Whoever got the cucumbers to market first earned the best prices; when the supply became a glut in the late summer, prices would plummet.

Quality had to be considered, too; peas and other early-season vegetables were always tastier if they were grown during the relatively cool days of early spring. For many crops, the best yields often came when a gentle snowfall followed the sowing. The even moisture resulted in terrific germination—far better than those years when hot and dry spring weather destroyed tender seedlings.

The price of a large, beautiful crop of vegetables is the same as that of freedom: eternal vigilance, or at least season-long vigilance. Watering was paramount. It was Mom's favourite job, and she took it very seriously. I, on the other hand, was fascinated by threats to the vegetable crop, weeds and bugs in particular. It didn't take long to learn that once either had a toehold, it was very difficult to eradicate them. Early detection is the key to controlling pests and weeds; spotting and uprooting them early in the game always pays large dividends.

By the time Bill and I reached our teens, helping Mom and Dad take care of the vegetable fields was a deeply ingrained part of our lives. Harvest time was the annual culmination of our collective efforts. We were accompanied by many of our friends, including Dave Grice and my future sister-in-law Valerie. (Both are still key members of the Hole's business, and Valerie chooses the vegetable varieties we grow each year.) We used to spend long summer days bent over in the fields, harvesting cabbage, hacking at the stems with long, sharp knives. (I still have a scar on one finger, a souvenir of a moment of carelessness.) We tossed the cabbages into the back of an old pick-up truck and listened to football games on the truck's radio: CBC for the University of Alberta Golden Bears games, CJCA for the Eskimos. We'd

Jim Hole with Lord Strathcona, inspecting seedling flats.

come down from the field covered in dust and sweat, but even our aching muscles didn't usually deter us from playing a game or two of football after we'd wolfed down one of Mom's dinners.

But my clearest, if not fondest, memories of harvest time revolve around carrots. We used pitchforks to dig up carrots, one at a time, then tied the bunches with binder twine as if we were cowboys roping calves. It was a painful job, and our hands developed thick calluses from the constant friction of the twine. I was ecstatic when we moved into the wholesale carrot business, since it meant that we would be forced to purchase a mechanical harvester to handle the incredible volume. That machine could harvest ten tons of carrots in fifteen minutes, and it still makes me shake my head a little, remembering all the effort we went through just to harvest a few hundred pounds.

The harvest is still one of my favourite times of year. I can't wait for the late summer to arrive, just so that I can wander into the cornfield and tear off a cob or two of a new variety for a quick taste test.

The Structure of Vegetable Gardening

My mother and I use different, but complementary, approaches to vegetable gardening. Mom relies mostly on experience, repeating the methods that worked in the past and discarding those that didn't. I like to mix science with art, turning to books, research reports, conferences, and my own studies at university to explain why vegetables grow the way they do. If you pay careful attention to your own experience and rely on the knowledge you glean from books and fellow gardeners, you'll rarely stumble.

The Basics

Great vegetable gardens are built from the ground up. To achieve high yields, great flavour, and good-looking vegetables, you need good soil, properly drained and rich in nutrients. Of course, not all vegetables are best suited to a rich loam, the soil commonly regarded as ideal. Rutabagas, for example, can be grown in clay soil. The yields will be reduced, but they develop gorgeous, smooth skins that really add to the aesthetic appeal of the vegetable.

Choosing Vegetables

With such a multitude of vegetable varieties to choose from, selecting the best seeds or seedlings for your garden can seem overwhelming. But by following a few simple guidelines, you can fill your plot with just the right vegetables to produce a bumper crop of perfect proportions. Know your climate and learn what a healthy seedling should look like on the greenhouse shelf. Tall, lanky, stretched seedlings have been starved for light and should be passed by in favour of stocky, robust seedlings that have enjoyed healthy light and nutrient levels.

Planting

Among the many lessons Mom taught me about vegetable gardening, these are the two most important: plant early, and start with the highest-quality seed or seedlings. Most Canadians still seem to think of the Victoria Day weekend as the starting line for the gardening season, but the truth is, for many crops that's far too late to take full advantage of the growing season. Worried about a spring frost? Don't be. A light frost won't hurt seed in the soil, and many young seedlings are remarkably frost tolerant.

The Growing Season

As anyone who has planted vegetables knows, there's a lot to do during the growing season. Watering, weeding, fertilizing, and keeping an eye out for pests keeps gardeners busy all season long. But somehow, when you're raising vegetables, these jobs seem more like recreation than a chore. At least, that's true most of the time—if you've ever tried to harvest potatoes after a hard rain, when the soil has turned to mud, you know how the curses can fly. But watching the growing season is one of the joys of gardening, when life bursts forth from the earth with such astonishing vigour.

But vegetable gardens are heaven for more than just us. They're also home to a wide array of pests. Think of it from their perspective: a vegetable garden is one big smorgasbord. You can fight off pests with sprays or biocontrols like pest-eating ladybugs, but I've always found that the most effective means of troubleshooting is to avoid stressing your plants. Keep them well fed and well watered, and make sure they've been planted in a location amenable to their particular light preference. A healthy plant can fend off pests far better than one that is already fighting neglect.

Vegetable Varieties

Each vegetable offers its own specific challenges and rewards, from forking carrots to bolting broccoli. Back when we were growing and selling whole-sale vegetables, we were often plagued by young cauliflower that would form small curds while still in the seedling flats and then fail to grow once transplanted into the field. I eventually learned that cauliflower responds to root crowding by attempting to form flowers: the curds. We gave our cauliflower transplants more room to grow, and the problem was solved.

Chemical Reactions

People are becoming more conscious of pesticide use, and that's a positive trend, as long as gardeners take a balanced approach. For us, pest control always begins with regular inspection of our plants. Pest problems are easier to handle if they are caught early, before the bug population explodes. Sometimes bugs are few enough in number that you can simply pick them off with your fingers.

If pesticides must be used, start with the least potent. Insecticidal soaps are a good place to start; they're effective on a wide range of insect pests, and you don't have to worry about eating the plants you've treated. If stronger pesticides like diazinon are called for, read and follow the label! Don't over-apply pesticide, and buy only what you need. A garage full of half-empty pesticide containers is unsafe and wasteful.

The best way to prevent pest and disease problems is to raise healthy, stress-free plants. That means keeping them well watered, weeded, and fertilized. Robust plants are far more capable of fighting off problems than are those that have been neglected!

Over the years I've learned a lot from Mom and Dad, from professional and amateur gardeners, vegetable researchers, and from the vegetables themselves. The most important lesson I've learned is that, as gardeners, we have to use the experience we've won while always being prepared to explore the new. The vegetable garden still holds many secrets, and I'm grateful that there will always be new mysteries to unearth.

CHAPTER 1 ❧
THE BASICS

*The key to successful vegetable gardening
lies right at your feet: the soil. We've
always been careful to replenish our garden soils by working in organic matter
every year. That can be a sweaty, time-
consuming job if you have a
big plot, but well worth the effort.
Replenished soils will reward you
with fewer pest troubles and high
yields of juicy, succulent vegetables.*

Definitions

What is a vegetable?

Lois ❖ This seems like a simple question, but it's not! According to the dictionary, a vegetable is any herbaceous plant that is wholly or partly edible. Many plants we think of as vegetables, such as tomatoes and pumpkins, are technically fruits, while others, such as corn, are grains. For the sake of this book, we're going to define vegetables as the less-sweet, more fibre-rich portions of plants grown specifically for their food value and flavour—and commonly eaten before dessert!

Jim ❖ The question gets more interesting when it comes to buying, selling, and processing produce. For example, in an 1893 decision about import duties, the US Supreme Court legally declared tomatoes to be vegetables. But botanically, there is no precise distinction between fruits and vegetables.

Soil

How do I prepare a new vegetable garden?

Lois ❖ Although it may seem like a lot of extra work initially, the preparation of your vegetable garden is the single most important factor in determining your success. Preparing a vegetable garden is much like preparing any other garden. Your primary goals are to enrich the soil with organic matter, loosen compacted soil, and eliminate as many weeds as possible. If you start with a clean bed, you'll save yourself countless hours of weeding in the future.

Jim ❖ Every year you should add organic matter (peat moss, compost, or well-rotted manure) to the soil. You should also dig or rototill the soil at least 15 cm deep, creating a loose soil bed that will encourage deep rooting.

Avoid the temptation to be overzealous with rich composts or manure in tomato plots and potato patches. If you give these crops an overly rich mixture of organic matter, the excess nitrogen will encourage leafy growth at the expense of fruit or tuber production. Fresh manure may also encourage the growth of scab on potatoes. Root crops also dislike excessive nitrogen; for example, carrots may form forked roots and rutabagas may split. So be generous with the organic matter, but aim for balance.

Why is good soil so important?

Lois ❖ Good soil is the foundation of a good garden. Grab a fistful of your soil and give it a squeeze. Does it hold together or fall apart? If it holds together, is it still soft and springy or does it feel like a lump of clay? What colour is it? If you have a nice, dark clump of earth that you can easily crumble between your fingers, you're well on your way. If your soil does not have these characteristics, your first step should be to improve your soil quality.

Jim ❖ You simply can't grow a successful garden in poor soil. Creating and maintaining good loam may take some work, but no gardening job is more important. Organic matter contributes to the *tilth* (physical condition) of the soil. Soil structure and texture have a direct effect on the water- and oxygen-holding capacity as well as on the soil micro-organisms. Crusting and puddling on the soil surface indicate poor tilth.

What is good soil?

Lois ❖ Soil—both garden soil and potting soil—should serve your plants' needs. Good soil anchors the roots firmly, but is loose and porous enough to allow them to grow and branch extensively. It retains moisture, but has adequate drainage. It's neither too acidic nor too alkaline, and contains all the nutrients your plants require.

Jim ❖ Good soil has excellent tilth, which is largely due to a high content of organic matter. The absolute lowest levels of organic matter that vegetables can tolerate is 1 percent; 6–7 percent is better, and many of our fields had 10–15 percent when we were growing vegetables.

Typical rooting depths of vegetables

Shallow (45–60 cm)	Moderate (90–120 cm)	Deep (120+ cm)
broccoli	bean, bush	artichoke
Brussels sprouts	bean, pole	asparagus
cabbage	beet	bean, lima
cauliflower	cucumber	parsnip
celery	eggplant	pumpkin
Chinese cabbage	pea	squash, winter
corn	pepper	sweet potato
endive	rutabaga	tomato
garlic	squash, summer	
leek	turnip	
lettuce		
onion		
parsley		
potato		
spinach		

'Gypsy' sweet pepper

What type of soil do vegetables need?

Lois ❖ Most vegetables prefer well-drained, rich, balanced soil.

Jim ❖ Well-drained, rich, and balanced mean:

- Well-drained: able to hold adequate moisture, while allowing any excess to drain away;
- Rich: lots of organic matter, whether from compost, manure, peat moss, or other sources;
- Balanced: pH neither too acidic nor too alkaline (6.0–7.5).

However, there are many exceptions to the rule. You must check the particular needs of every variety you plant. For instance, rutabaga, turnips, and kohlrabi actually grow better in soils that have modest levels of nitrogen.

How deep should the topsoil be?

Lois ❖ The deeper the topsoil the better, but you should start with at least 30 cm.

Jim ❖ Good, deep topsoil gives your vegetables more room to establish their roots. Deep, vigorous roots are important because they help plants to withstand drought. Some crops need a deep bed of soil. For example, carrots need 30–40 cm, depending on the variety, and parsnips can use up to 60 cm.

Why is good drainage important?

Lois ❖ If you don't have adequate drainage, your vegetables will literally drown. It's as simple as that.

Jim ❖ In poorly drained soil, the space between soil particles fills with water rather than air. Roots need oxygen to grow and thrive, and a poorly drained soil contains very little oxygen and too much moisture.

Many beneficial soil organisms can't survive in waterlogged soils. Various bacteria and fungi in the soil break down organic matter into nutrients for your vegetables to absorb. Without these nutrients, the plants eventually starve.

How can I tell whether my soil has proper drainage?

Lois ❖ If your soil has proper drainage, water won't stay on its surface for long. It will be absorbed quickly—you can watch it disappear into the soil in just a few minutes.

Jim ❖ Dig a hole 20–30 cm deep, fill it with water, and watch. The water should drain away slowly but steadily, leaving the hole empty within an hour. If the water just sits, the drainage is poor. Work in plenty of organic matter to improve soil drainage.

Moisture-holding capacities

Soil Type	Maximum water-holding capacity (kg) per 100 kg of soil
Sandy	6
Sandy Loam	14
Loam	22
Clay Loam	27
Silty Loam	31
Clay	35

i.e., 100 kg of sandy soil can hold 6 kg of water when the soil is completely saturated.

On the other hand, if the water drains out of the hole almost immediately, you have excessively porous or sandy soil. This won't necessarily harm your plants, but it does mean you'll have to water and fertilize more frequently.

How do I correct soil that drains too quickly?

Lois ❖ The best solution is to add organic matter: well-rotted manure, compost, or peat moss, for example.

Jim ❖ Regularly adding organic matter to the soil will help you strike the right balance between drainage and water retention. Organic material causes the soil mineral particles to *flocculate* (stick together) into larger, distinct particles. Soil has a granular structure, and larger grains allow roots and air to penetrate the soil more easily. Organic matter also holds water.

Does rototilling damage the texture of the soil?

Jim ❖ Excessive rototilling pulverizes the soil. The finer the soil particles, the greater the potential wind and water erosion. Pulverized soils are also more prone to compacting.

Soil Tests

What is a soil test? Can I do it myself?

Lois ❖ A simple soil test is a standardized method of measuring the various nutritional components that make up your soil and determining your soil pH. There are also more sophisticated tests that will provide you with micronutrient levels and level of soil salts. The more-detailed tests are generally used by commercial growers. For a home gardener, a basic soil test is usually adequate.

You can perform a reasonably accurate soil pH and nutrient test yourself. Kits are available from most garden centres.

Should I get my soil tested?

Lois ❖ You should get your soil tested if you have a very large garden or acreage or if you have a history of plants growing poorly in a specific area of your garden despite proper care.

Jim ❖ If you have specific problem areas in your garden, it's a good idea to get a soil test. You can learn as much from a soil test as you would from several years of trial and error. If your garden is large or has distinct soil pockets, you may need to perform several tests. Take a core sample 15 cm into the topsoil. Take samples from different spots in your garden and mix them. This way you get a more representative, and more accurate, measure of your garden.

What does a soil test tell me?

Jim ❖ A basic soil test tells you several things:

- Levels of the major nutrients: nitrogen (N), phosphate (P), and potash (K). These nutrients are represented by the numbers on a fertilizer label; that is, 10-52-10 means 10 percent nitrogen, 52 percent phosphate, and 10 percent potash. Sulphur levels are also sometimes included.
- pH level: the soil's acidity or basicity.
- Level of soluble salts: plants burn if the concentration is too high.
- Soil texture: the relative quantities of sand, silt, clay, and organic matter.

An advanced soil test may include the levels of the other essential plant nutrients: iron, molybdenum, sulphur, magnesium, calcium, zinc, copper, and boron.

For farmers, it can be very expensive not to test soil. For example, a deficiency of 20 kg of nitrogen per hectare adds up to a 10,000-kg shortage on a 500-hectare farm. That shortfall could result in catastrophic crop-yield losses. Thankfully, the stakes aren't as high for home gardeners. However, if you're having trouble growing healthy plants, it's worth spending a few dollars to test your soil.

Should I test the pH of the soil in my garden?

Lois ❖ Yes. Test your soil pH every two years, more often if you are experiencing problems.

Jim ❖ Soil pH strongly influences how well your vegetables absorb nutrients, and it also affects the health of the soil microbial population. In short, a pH that's too high or too low leads to an unhealthy garden.

It's important that you test the overall soil, not just a single spot. To do this, take a small trowel and dig down 15 cm into the soil. Put the sample in a bucket, then move on. Take half a dozen samples like this from the area of your garden that you want to test, and blend them to make a single, representative sample.

Our vegetable garden.

Why is my soil's pH important?

Lois ❖ pH affects both your garden's yield and the flavour of your vegetables. To produce the best, tastiest vegetables, keep an eye on pH!

Jim ❖ First, let's review our chemistry. pH is a scale for measuring acids and bases. On this scale, 7.0 is neutral—neither acidic nor alkaline. (Water is normally pH 7.0.) As the numbers go down (6.9, 6.8, etc.), the acidity increases. As the numbers rise (7.1, 7.2, etc.), the alkalinity increases.

In alkaline soil, many essential nutrients remain bound up as insoluble compounds. This means that your plants have a harder time absorbing them from the soil. If the plant can't absorb enough of the essential nutrients, its yield and quality is reduced.

Most vegetables perform best in slightly acidic soil (6.2–6.5). However, when the pH is too low, plants tend to absorb excessive quantities of trace elements, particularly metals like iron and zinc, which can be toxic. As well, many beneficial soil micro-organisms, which convert elements like nitrogen into forms that plants can use, cannot survive in very acidic soils.

How do I adjust my soil's pH?

Lois ❖ Assuming you have tested your soil's pH, take the results to a good garden centre. A staff member should be able to give you reliable advice on which amendments to add to improve your soil's pH.

Jim ❖ To adjust the pH, you must amend the soil. Sulphur lowers the soil's pH (making it more acidic), while horticultural lime raises the pH (making it more alkaline). You can purchase these products at most garden centres.

If you're adding sulphur, stick with very fine sulphur or aluminum sulphate: coarse sulphur reacts too slowly to benefit your vegetable garden. Use dolomitic lime, because it contains both calcium and magnesium (two important plant nutrients). Be sure to buy a fine grade of lime that will react quickly in the soil.

How much sulphur/lime to add to soil to change pH levels

GARDEN SULPHUR* kg/100 m² (to lower pH)

Desired pH Change	Sands	Loam	Clay
8.5–6.5	23	29	34
8.0–6.5	14	17	23
7.5–6.5	6	9	12
7.0–6.5	1	2	3

* although sulphur is effective, it is slow to react in soil

LIMESTONE kg/100 m² (to increase pH)

Desired pH Change	Sandy loam	Loam	Silt Loam	Clay
4.0–6.5	58	80	97	115
4.5–6.5	48	67	97	115
5.0–6.5	39	53	64	76
5.5–6.5	30	39	46	53
6.0–6.5	16	22	25	28

Adding to the Soil

Can I improve the quality of my soil, or is it best to remove it and bring in new topsoil?

Lois ❖ Unless your soil is absolutely dreadful, there's no reason to start entirely from scratch. Add peat moss, well-rotted manure, and compost to help improve your soil.

Jim ❖ If you have extremely poor soil, invest in a load of good topsoil. You'll save yourself an awful lot of hard work and frustration.

Buy your soil only from a reputable dealer. Look for soil rich in organic matter, with a fairly loose texture. ·

Should I add anything to the soil in an established vegetable garden?

Lois ❖ Even if you're blessed with good soil, you still have to work to maintain it. Add organic matter every fall and spring, if possible. I like to rototill the remains of my vegetables back in the garden every fall.

Jim ❖ Rich topsoil is best and easiest, but well–rotted manure, compost, leaf mold, peat moss, and fertilizers also help to improve your soil.

Why do gardeners add manure to their soil?

Lois ❖ Manure is one of many types of organic matter that can be used to condition the soil and add nutrients. Manure keeps soil from becoming dense and unproductive. As the manure breaks down, it releases nutrients.

Jim ❖ Manure provides a slow-release source of nutrients while greatly improving soil texture. Soil micro-organisms break down the manure, and as they die they release important plant nutrients such as nitrogen. The broken-down manure improves soil structure by "gluing" soil particles together and allowing air, water and roots to penetrate the spaces.

However, fresh manure contains high levels of salts (for example, ammonium) that can burn plant roots. Always use only well-rotted (composted) manure to avoid salt problems.

Does it matter what kind of manure I use (sheep, steer, etc.)?

Jim ❖ Manure varies in composition somewhat from animal to animal (see following table), but you can use any type. Just remember to use well-composted manure.

Typical Composition of Manures

Source	Dry Matter (%)	Approximate Composition (% dry weight)		
		N	P_2O_5	K_2O
Dairy	15–25	0.6–2.1	0.7–1.1	2.4–3.6
Feedlot	20–40	1.0–2.5	0.9–1.6	2.4–3.6
Horse	15–25	1.7–3.0	0.7–1.2	1.2–2.2
Poultry	20–30	2.0–4.5	4.5–6.0	1.2–2.4
Sheep	25–35	3.0–4.0	1.2–1.6	3.0–4.0
Swine	20–30	3.0–4.0	0.4–0.6	0.5–1.0

Can I add mushroom manure to a vegetable garden?

Jim ❖ Yes, but use it sparingly. Mushroom manure is a "hot" source of nutrients, meaning that it has a high salt level, which can burn plants, particularly young plants and seedlings. If you want to use it, apply a thin layer (1 cm) to the soil annually and work it in thoroughly.

Does adding perlite to clay-like garden soil help it drain better? Is it the best solution for poor drainage?

Lois ❖ It's one solution, but it's not the best or cheapest alternative. It's also very dusty. You'd be better off adding peat moss, manure, and/or compost.

Jim ❖ Perlite does help clay soil to drain better. However, perlite particles aren't very strong and can break down very quickly, especially if you work the soil with a rototiller. The other problem with perlite is that you need a tremendous amount to improve drainage, which is very expensive. It also blows away very easily in light winds. Instead, I recommend using plenty of organic matter. It's far cheaper, lasts much longer, and improves the soil texture.

I think that my soil is deficient in iron. What should I do?

Jim ❖ If you're really worried, you might consider investing in a soil test. However, if you believe your plants aren't absorbing enough iron, the problem might just be the pH of your soil. If your soil is too alkaline, the iron won't be available for absorption by plant roots.

Iron in alkaline soil is comparable to sugar in an ice-cold glass of water— it's not very soluble. Lowering the soil's pH is like warming up that glass of water: the lower the pH, the more easily iron is absorbed.

If your soil has a high pH, lower it with aluminum sulphate or very fine sulphur. You can also add chelated iron to the soil. In alkaline soil, chelated iron works much better than regular iron.

What should I do about evergreen needles in my garden? Is there any way to neutralize the acidity from the needles?

Lois ❖ Lime counteracts the acidity of the needles. It would take an awful lot of evergreen needles, however, to significantly lower a soil's pH. Test your soil before assuming that acidity is the problem.

Jim ❖ The area under an evergreen tree is a difficult place to grow plants for many reasons. So if you plant your garden near an evergreen tree and it does poorly, don't necessarily blame the needles! Acidity is often not the problem. The thick, dense canopy of an evergreen is shady, and its roots absorb a great deal of water. Even if the pH is perfectly balanced, you'll have a hard time growing any kind of plant under or near your tree.

My neighbour heard that adding sulphur to the garden will help her plants. What effect does sulphur have?

Lois ❖ Your neighbour is right—*if* the soil is too alkaline. Adding the correct amount of sulphur will reduce the soil pH to the ideal range for plant growth.

Jim ❖ You can add sulphur for two reasons: to lower the soil pH or to increase the amount of sulphur in sulphur-deficient soils. The sulphur you add must be very fine (microfine or superfine) in order to react quickly with your soil. It can take months for coarse sulphur to break down in your soil. Use aluminum sulphate or iron sulphate, which react quickly with the soil.

Should I add lime to my soil?

Lois ❖ Lime doesn't solve all gardening problems, but it is good for neutralizing acidic soils. If you're adding the lime directly into your garden, do it in the fall after everything's cleaned up, or else first thing in the spring.

Jim ❖ Lime adjusts the pH of soil by neutralizing the acidity of components like peat moss. There's no reason to add lime, however, unless your soil is too acidic.

I have a new garden on heavy clay soil with some good compost on top. A friend recommended adding worms to improve the overall soil mix. Will this help?

Lois ❖ If you have lots of worms in your garden, it indicates that you have healthy soil. Worm castings are actually sold as a soil amendment at most garden centres. Adding worms to your soil certainly won't hurt, but you also need lots (at least a 50-cm layer) of rich compost or high-quality topsoil. The worms will contribute to the ongoing conditioning of your garden soil, but they can't improve it by themselves.

CHAPTER 2 ❧
CHOOSING VEGETABLES

*Back in the 1950s, we grew a corn
variety called 'Alta Sweet,' the only one
at the time with a growing period short
enough to mature before the fall frost.
But the early maturation date was its
only real advantage: the corn was fit only
for cattle feed as far as we were concerned.
Thankfully, there are now many great
corn varieties that will grow to full
maturity right across Canada. And the
same is true for peppers, melons,
and a number of other heat-loving
crops once considered too tender to
grow in Canada. The lesson here?
Choose your varieties carefully, to
suit your requirements for light, heat,
length of season, and, of course, taste.*

Climate

What is a zone?

Lois ❖ Zones are regions that have similar climates. The lower the zone number, the colder the average winter temperatures. Zone 10 is frost-free year-round, while zone 0 has permafrost. Canada is unusual because of its wide range of climatic zones: Victoria is zone 9, while Resolute Bay is zone 0.

Jim ❖ Zone ratings are used as a guideline for determining whether a plant will survive in a particular region. But zone maps don't apply to most vegetables because zones are largely based on winter low temperatures. However, for a few perennial vegetables, such as Jerusalem artichoke and asparagus, zones do apply.

The most important climate considerations for vegetables are sunlight (duration and intensity), rainfall, day and night temperatures, and frost-free period.

What is a growing season?

Lois ❖ In general terms, the growing season refers to the period each year that is suitable for the active growth of plants. In specific terms, it is the number of frost-free days in a given area. You can extend your growing season by using devices like hot caps, row coverings, and cold frames.

'Green Globe' artichoke

How do I know whether a vegetable will grow in my climate?

Lois ❖ You'll never really know until you try. Don't be afraid to experiment! If you have the time and the inclination, a three-year trial will give you a good indication of how well a vegetable will perform in a given climate. Your local garden centre should also be able to recommend varieties that will succeed in your region.

Jim ❖ This question is more complex than it seems. Some vegetables simply won't mature from seed if you plant them in a particular region. Tomatoes, for example, won't mature from seed if you sow them directly into the soil in most parts of Canada. You must start them from transplants.

Others plants might survive but will not thrive. Okra, for instance, will survive in a cooler growing season, but produce very few fruit. Other vegetables, like melons, may produce a good crop only once every few years in a cooler climate.

Is it worth growing these more challenging vegetables? In my opinion, yes, but not everyone would agree. So, seek advice from experienced gardeners in your region, but at the same time don't let fear of failure prevent you from experimenting.

Is our growing season long enough to produce big watermelons, pumpkins and artichokes?

Lois ❖ In most parts of Canada, you're better off treating watermelons as a novelty crop: they're tough to grow in a short-season area. Pumpkins fare quite a bit better, and do well in most regions. Artichokes grow remarkably quickly from transplants and mature in early summer.

Another point to remember is that there are many different varieties of each vegetable. Varieties have different maturity dates, and some are better suited to areas with short growing seasons.

Jim ❖ Watermelons and pumpkins (to a lesser extent) require lots of heat. To increase plant growth and hasten maturity, cover the plants with a woven, lightweight fabric at night and during cooler weather. And of course, you must give the plants every possible advantage, such as starting from large, sturdy seedlings and using hot caps or row coverings to extend the season.

Shopping for Seeds and Transplants

What factors should I consider when choosing vegetable varieties?

Lois ❖ Each year I like to grow some of my old favourites, that is, varieties we have tested and grown in the garden. I also like to try a few new varieties each year. New varieties are being developed all the time, and staff at your local garden centre should be able to recommend suitable ones.

Consider the characteristics that matter to you, such as heritage varieties, novelty, disease and pest resistance, flavour, productivity, and storage. Read current publications, talk to other gardeners, visit your garden centre, and above all, don't be afraid to experiment.

What features should I look for in a greenhouse or garden centre?

Lois ❖ Look for one feature above all others when shopping for vegetable seeds and transplants: cleanliness. It doesn't much matter whether the greenhouse or garden centre is ultra-modern, but a dirty facility increases your chances of taking home serious diseases or insect pests.

Jim ❖ Beyond cleanliness, look for knowledgeable staff, a good selection and healthy plants. Avoid soft, overgrown plants that haven't been acclimatized to outdoor conditions: they will have a difficult time becoming established in the garden.

While shopping, how do I recognize which plants are healthy?

Lois ❖ Healthy transplants are firm, robust plants with dark green leaves. Never buy plants that are stretched or crowded. Poor plants are pale and gangly, with tall, weak stems and small leaves—these are plants to avoid!

Why are some vegetables sold in packs of six or four, and others in pots?

Lois ❖ This is determined partly by consumer demand and partly by the fact that some vegetables outgrow packs and are better suited to pots.

Jim ❖ If you look at tomatoes, for example, some people prefer to buy several smaller tomatoes, rather than few, bigger tomatoes. Four larger tomato plants might be the same price as six smaller ones. The larger tomatoes might produce fruit more quickly, with more fruit per plant, but the smaller ones may ultimately produce more fruit because you have two extra plants.

Some vegetables, like corn, simply grow too quickly to do well in small packs. Once they overgrow their containers, they will never grow into large mature cob-producing plants no matter how well you treat them. Other vegetables, such as onions, do well with multiple seedlings in a pack. Once you separate the seedlings and give them space to grow, they'll develop properly.

'July Gold' corn

How many vegetable plants do I need to fill in a specific area? Is there an overall formula?

Lois ❖ There are no hard and fast rules. Some gardeners like to grow plants in rows for ease of harvest and cultivation. Others grow vegetables in blocks to maximize production per unit of area. It's up to your individual judgement.

Jim ❖ Although there are no hard and fast rules, you should follow some guidelines to give your plants enough space for good production. For example, you can space cauliflower fairly tightly—perhaps 15 cm between plants within the row and 60 to 70 cm between rows. Melons, on the other hand, require more space and should have at least 20 to 30 cm between plants within the row and at least 180 cm between rows. The seed packages or plant tags will provide you with reliable guidelines.

Average and good yields

The figures below represent the rough yield (in kilograms) of a standard garden plot (5 metres by 5 metres). The chart has been compiled for comparative purposes only, to suggest how vegetables typically produce and to show how much conditions can influence the harvest. These figures are intended only as a guideline, not a guarantee, and cannot account for the many variables that affect individual gardens, such as local weather, soil quality, seed quality, and variety traits.

Vegetable	Average	Good
artichoke	35	44
aspargus	9	14
bean	13	36
beet	52	73
broccoli	36	45
Brussels sprouts	52	64
cabbage	88	109
carrots	95	127
cauliflower	39	58
celery	200	255
corn	29	45
cucumber	43	91
eggplant	70	91
garlic	47	60
lettuce	78	190
onion	124	182
pea	14	23
pepper, sweet	37	73
pepper, hot	14	23
potato	105	145
spinach	30	58
tomato	85	99

I'm eager to begin enjoying garden vegetables as quickly as possible. Which ones mature earliest?

Lois ❖ One of the earliest-maturing vegetables is spinach, followed closely by radishes and leaf lettuce. I like to sow my lettuce fairly thickly. Then I thin the patch by harvesting as soon as the young plants are few centimetres high. That way I have fresh garden lettuce by mid spring and am creating space for the remaining plants to grow.

I also like to "push the envelope" somewhat. I always plant a few seeds of each crop early in the spring. (I seed a little thicker when I'm planting early.) I have lost some seedlings to frost and cool weather, but more often than not I'm enjoying fresh beans and new potatoes weeks before my neighbours. Given the low cost of a few seeds, I always say, "Live dangerously!"

Days to maturity under optimum growing conditions

Vegetable	Early	Late
bean, bush	48	60
bean, pole	62	68
beet	56	70
*broccoli	55	78
*Brussels sprouts	90	100
cabbage	62	120
carrots	50	95
*cauliflower	50	125
*celery	90	125
chard, Swiss	50	60
Chinese cabbage	70	80
corn	64	95
cucumber, pickling	48	58
cucumber, slicing	62	72
eggplant	50	80
kohlrabi	50	60
lettuce, head	70	85
lettuce, leaf	40	50
onion, dry	90	150
onion, green	45	60
pea	56	75
*pepper, hot	65	80
*pepper, sweet	65	80
potato	90	120
pumpkin	100	120
radish	22	30
spinach	37	45
squash, summer	40	50
squash, winter	85	110
*tomato	60	90
turnip	40	75

This figure represents the number of days from transplanting an established seedling.

What is a winter vegetable?

Lois ❖ Winter vegetables are vegetables that store well. They're wonderful because they you can eat them all winter long. Winter vegetables include onions, potatoes, rutabagas, carrots, cabbage, and winter squash.

Jim ❖ Winter vegetables can tolerate low storage temperatures. Cool storage slows down their respiration rate and helps them maintain their moisture and stored energy, so they will last many weeks or months after harvest.

What is an ornamental vegetable? Are they edible?

Lois ❖ An ornamental vegetable is a variety that is particularly—sometimes unusually—attractive. Most ornamental vegetables are edible, and some very tasty. But others are best left as decoration—there is a difference between edible and palatable!

Some of the most beautiful ornamentals vegetables include Bright Lights Swiss chard, scarlet runner beans, decorative lettuces, and kale (both ornamental and garden varieties). But if you ask me, nearly all vegetables have ornamental value. For instance, there are few sights more beautiful than row upon row of corn just before harvest—and the leftover stalks make great Halloween decorations!

Choosing for Specific Situations

How do I make the best use of our horrible little plot?

Lois ❖ I'll assume that by "horrible" you mean you have poor soil and little light. If the soil is extremely poor, the simplest solution is to add a nice load of high-quality topsoil. A 15-cm layer spread around your entire plot is good; double that is better. If the soil is marginal, add lots of well-rotted manure, compost, peat moss, or a combination of all three.

As far as light goes, trim back any trees that block the sun. If your vegetable garden is more important to you than the trees, you might even consider removing them. All vegetables require full sun to do well, but a few, such as leaf lettuce, spinach, and green onions, will tolerate some shade. They won't grow as vigorously, but they will survive.

Jim ❖ There are also ingenious ways to make a garden work in almost any situation. Be selective with your planting: don't try growing corn or cucumbers if heat and light pose a problem. Instead, try less fussy crops like peas, carrots, radishes, and lettuce. You can also try container gardening. Tomatoes, cucumbers, beans, and mesclun grow well in containers. You can even grow potatoes in barrels!

What vegetables grow well in clay soil?

Lois ❖ I've always found that rutabaga, turnips and kohlrabi actually grow fairly well in heavier clay soils. The skins are much smoother, with no cracks, and they suffer far fewer injuries from root maggots.

Jim ❖ Rather than trying to match vegetables to poor soil, take a few simple steps to amend it (see chapter 1, Soil).

Which vegetables grow well in shady areas?

Lois ❖ Leafy vegetables, including lettuce, spinach, and Swiss chard, will tolerate partial shade. However, full sun from morning till evening is best for all vegetables, and especially for fruiting plants.

Jim ❖ Put shade-loving bedding plants and perennials into those shady areas, and plant your vegetables in the sun! Most fruiting vegetables require at least five hours of afternoon sunlight. Full sun all day is best. Your yields will go down proportionately with lower light levels or shorter day lengths.

Are there any drought-tolerant vegetables?

Lois ❖ Some vegetables will tolerate occasionally dry soil, but that doesn't mean that they perform well in it! A plant may tolerate some stress, but its yield may be reduced in response. Try to keep your vegetable garden watered properly at all times.

Jim ❖ Most deep-rooted vegetables can withstand drought fairly well—parsnips and carrots, for example.

Are there any perennial vegetables?

Lois ❖ Absolutely! A well-established asparagus patch will produce spears every spring for decades. Other perennial vegetables include horseradish and Jerusalem artichoke. Be sure to mark the perennial areas of your garden carefully. You don't want to tear up any emerging plants when you rototill in the spring!

Jim ❖ Many other vegetables are biennials. For example, take carrots and parsnips. In the first growing season, they produce their long tap roots. If they continued growing for a second season, a seed stalk would emerge from the crown. Occasionally a cold spell during the first growing season will trigger these crops to produce seed.

I want to let my children have their own area in the garden this year. What vegetables should they plant?

Lois ❖ Great idea! Your best choices for a children's garden are plants with large seeds, limited care requirements, and a solid success rate. Beans, peas, carrots, radishes, sunflowers, kohlrabi, and pumpkin are all good choices. Tomato transplants are also excellent.

Jim ❖ For a better chance of success, choose proven, disease-resistant varieties with a shorter growing season.

I only have a balcony, but I would love to grow some vegetables. Which ones are best for container growing?

Lois ❖ I've heard of people growing almost everything on their balconies! You're only limited by the amount of available space and light. The best candidates for container growing are beans, cucumbers, eggplant, garlic, leaf lettuce, peppers, spinach, and tomatoes.

Are any vegetables or their parts poisonous?

Jim ❖ Very few. Rhubarb leaves contain toxic compounds called oxalates. Never eat rhubarb leaves. You should also avoid potato tubers that have turned green after being exposed to light. They contain poisonous alkaloids. Tomato and potato leaves also contain alkaloids and should never be eaten.

Strangely enough, almost every plant we eat contains naturally occurring poisonous compounds. However, these chemicals are harmless in the servings we normally consume. For example, cauliflower produces compounds called glucosinates that, if consumed in large quantities, can be poisonous. On the bright side, you would need to consume about a wheelbarrow full of cauliflower at a single sitting to endanger your health.

CHAPTER 3 ❧
PLANTING

*Once, during the early days of market
gardening, we made the mistake of
buying hundreds of pounds of cheap
corn seed. We thought we'd found a
bargain, but when only a dismal
percentage of the seeds germinated, we
learned the disappointing truth: cheap
seed is no bargain if it rots in the soil.
Beware bargain-basement seed.
A slightly bigger investment initially
will reap large dividends
at harvest time.*

Direct seeding vegetables

What is direct seeding?
What vegetables are best seeded this way?

Lois ❖ Direct seeding, or direct sowing, simply means putting the seed directly in the soil, as opposed to growing it in a greenhouse and then transplanting it to the garden. Some vegetables grow best when direct seeded, including peas, carrots, beets, lettuce, radishes, and spinach. Others, such as tomatoes, peppers, and eggplant, should be transplanted.

Jim ❖ Direct seeding will be most successful under when the soil is at a optimal temperature and sufficient moisture, oxygen, and micronutrients are available. If the soil is too cool, too hot, too wet, or too dry, the germination rate will be lowered; under extreme conditions, the seeds may not germinate at all. As well, many plants are slow to germinate and may not mature by the end of the growing season if they are seeded directly. For such varieties, transplanting is best.

Soil temperatures for seed germination (°C)

Vegetable	Minimum	Optimum range	Maximum
asparagus	10	16–29	35
bean	16	16–29	35
bean, lima	16	18–29	29
beet	4	10–29	35
cabbage	4	7–35	37
carrots	4	7–29	35
cauliflower	4	7–29	37
celery	4	16–21	29
corn	10	16–35	41
cucumber	16	16–35	41
eggplant	16	24–35	35
lettuce	2	4–27	29
okra	16	21–35	41
onion	2	10–35	35
parsnip	2	10–21	29
pea	4	4–24	29
pepper	16	18–35	35
pumpkin	16	21–32	37
radish	4	7–32	35
spinach	2	7–24	29
squash	16	21–35	37
Swiss chard	4	10–29	41
tomato	10	16–29	35
turnip	4	16–41	41

What vegetable seeds can be planted in the fall?

Lois ❖ You can plant many vegetables in the fall, including onions, lettuce, and parsnips. You will be rewarded with earlier growth in the spring— often a couple of weeks earlier than vegetables planted in the spring. The key is to plant late—just before freeze up—and to sow twice as thick as normal, since not all seed will survive the typical freezing, thawing and crusty soil of late winter and early spring.

Jim ❖ If you plant the seeds too early in the fall, some of them may germinate and then die during the winter. If you wait until just before freeze up, most of the seeds will survive. You're almost certain to lose a greater proportion of seeds sown in the fall, but you'll be compensated with an earlier harvest the following season.

Which vegetables can I plant earliest in the spring?

Lois ❖ Plant your onions, lettuce, parsnips, peas, and garlic as soon as you can work the soil. These vegetables will survive even a hard frost.

Jim ❖ The main goal of early planting is to get an early harvest. Plant your cool-season vegetables early, but also gamble with a few warmer-season vegetables. Yellow and green beans are good risks, but sow them a little thicker than you would later in the season. It's worth the risk, if you're a bit adventurous.

When is it too late to direct seed?

Lois ❖ It depends on the time required from sowing to harvest, and this varies with temperature. The warmer the weather, the quicker vegetables mature. Your timing also depends on the hardiness of the plant and your average first-frost date. If the mature plant can sustain some frost, you can push your planting dates a little later. For example, I like to plant assorted leaf lettuces as late as mid August. Although they may not mature fully, they will tolerate light frosts, and the cooler weather keeps them from going to seed. And I enjoy sweet, fresh lettuce right through the fall!

How do I test the viability of my vegetable seeds?

Lois ❖ Place ten or twenty seeds between two layers of moist paper towel, and keep the paper constantly moist and warm (20-24°C) for several days. Once the seeds have had time to germinate, count the number of seeds with sprouts versus the number without sprouts to estimate the percentage of viable seed.

Jim ❖ If the results leave you in doubt, get rid of the old seeds and buy fresh ones. It's a small investment when you consider all of the effort you're going to put into your garden.

Is there an easier way to sow seed than doing it by hand?

Lois ❖ If you find that the seeds stick together when you plant them by hand, try blending a little talcum powder in with them.

Jim ❖ Several seeders on the market can make sowing a lot easier. The simplest is a hand seeder that evenly meters out the seeds—much better than trying to pour them straight out of the package. The Saalet Seeder is a Danish seeder made of plastic that can be pushed down the rows. The different "plates" in the seeder can be matched to various seed sizes. Earthway is another mechanical seeder that can be pushed through the garden.

If I plant my seeds today and it gets cold tonight, will they freeze?

Lois ❖ Freezing night temperatures won't affect seeds, because they are naturally protected by the soil. However, once seedlings emerge, frost-sensitive vegetables can be injured by freezing temperatures.

Jim ❖ A night or two of frost won't hurt seeds protected beneath the soil, but prolonged cold spells can cause warm-season vegetable seeds to rot in the ground. That's why cucumbers often fail to emerge from the soil after a prolonged cold spell. And the only solution for that problem is to re-seed once the temperature is warmer.

I've heard that green potatoes are poisonous. Is it safe to plant green seed potatoes?

Lois ❖ Go ahead and plant them! They will grow into perfectly normal plants, and they certainly won't produce green tubers. I've planted green potatoes all my life, and I've never had a problem.

Jim ❖ Green potatoes contain elevated levels of toxic alkaloids, so you should never eat them. However, there's no reason not to plant green seed potatoes. The alkaloids won't move into the new tubers.

Potato tubers, like potato leaves, turn green in response to light. This problem usually occurs when the soil has eroded and exposed portions of the tubers in the ground. This is the reason we recommend hilling potatoes, that is, piling soil around the base of the plants. I like to hill the potatoes in mid June.

My garlic is sprouting. Can I plant it?

Lois ❖ Yes! Once a garlic bulb sprouts, you should either plant it or compost it. Fortunately, garlic is very frost tolerant. You can plant it as soon as the ground thaws in the spring. Some people even plant their garlic in the late fall, for an early summer harvest.

Jim ❖ Not all sprouting garlic is suitable for planting. If the shoots are excessively long, soft and pale, the bulb will be quite weak. Producing those shoots drains the bulb's stored nutrients. But if the shoots are small, go ahead and plant the bulb. If the shoots are long, plant new, healthy bulbs.

Do I need to transplant tomatoes and peppers grown in half-gallon pots?

Lois ❖ Yes. A pot of that size won't give the plants nearly enough room as they mature. I recommend at least a 15-litre pot for tomatoes and a 10-litre pot for peppers.

Jim ❖ If you leave the plants in small containers, their roots quickly become overgrown, filling in all the pore spaces in the soil. This leaves less space for air, water, and nutrients. It's virtually impossible to keep the soil moist and the plants well fed. The containers are also more likely to fall over in the wind. We use 20-litre containers for our mature tomatoes and peppers. It's well worth it!

I have a raised bed made out of railway ties. Is it safe to plant vegetables in it?

Lois ❖ If it makes you nervous, don't do it! I'd recommend that you avoid using railway ties in your vegetable garden. Many people worry that creosote—the black, tarry substance used in railway ties—might contaminate their vegetables. To be safe, replace the ties with untreated wood if you're going to grow food plants in this bed. Otherwise, grow non-edible plants, such as annuals or flowering perennials, in it.

Jim ❖ Health risks associated with railway ties (or any other toxic material) are ultimately linked to exposure. Cutting, handling, and touching ties increases exposure, for example. Well-weathered railway ties also contain less creosote than freshly treated ties, so there's obviously less exposure when you're using older ties. It makes sense to be cautious, even though several studies indicate that the movement of creosote into soil is minimal. Health Canada provides detailed information on several different preservatives and safe levels of exposure. My advice for your vegetable garden is to be conservative and use either untreated wood or wood treated with less toxic materials like Borax, Thompson's Water Seal, or copper naphthenate.

Starting Seeds Indoors

What do I need to start vegetables indoors?

Jim ❖ In addition to your seeds, you'll need seedling trays, grow lights (or a warm, sunny window), seedling mix, vermiculite, fertilizer, pest-control products, and a good misting bottle.

Days required for seedlings to emerge, by soil temperature (°C)

These figures are based on seed planted 1 cm deep; planting at greater depths delays emergence.

Vegetable	0	5	10	15	20	25	30	35	40
asparagus	0	0	53	24	15	10	12	20	28
bean, lima	—	—	0	31	18	7	7	0	—
bean, snap	0	0	0	16	11	8	6	6	0
beet	—	42	17	10	6	5	5	5	—
cabbage	—	—	15	9	6	5	4	—	—
carrots	0	51	17	10	7	6	6	9	0
cauliflower	—	—	20	10	6	5	5	—	—
celery	0	41	16	12	7	0	0	0	—
corn	0	0	22	12	7	4	4	3	0
cucumber	0	0	0	13	6	4	3	3	—
eggplant	—	—	—	—	13	8	5	—	—
lettuce	49	15	7	4	3	2	3	0	0
okra	0	0	0	27	17	13	7	6	7
onion	136	31	13	7	5	4	4	13	0
parsnip	172	57	27	19	14	15	32	0	0
pea	—	36	14	9	8	6	6	—	—
pepper	0	0	0	25	13	8	8	9	0
radish	0	29	11	6	4	4	3	—	—
spinach	63	23	12	7	6	5	6	0	0
tomato	0	0	43	14	8	6	6	9	0
turnip	0	0	5	3	2	1	1	1	3

'Red Ace' beets

When should I start my seeds indoors? Should I start some vegetables earlier than others?

Jim ❖ Your starting dates will vary, depending on the seed and your region. The chart below provides some basic guidelines.

When to start vegetables indoors

This chart shows approximately how long you need from seeding to transplanting in the garden. The periods in the brackets suggest the approximate relation to the average date of the last spring frost, which you will need to confirm for your area.

9–10 weeks (late February to early March)
celeriac, celery, peppers

7–8 weeks (mid March)
eggplant, leek, onion, tomato

2–4 weeks (early April)
broccoli, Brussels sprouts, cabbage, cauliflower, lettuce

0–2 weeks (late April to early May)
cucumbers, pumpkins, squash

'Utah 52-70' celery

How to start vegetable seeds indoors

- Fill a seedling flat to within 1 cm of the top with good-quality seedling mix, and wet the mix.
- Plant seeds shallowly: to about the depth of the seed's thickness.
- Plant 3 seeds in each cell for larger seeds, 8–10 seeds per cell for fine seeds.
- Cover the seeds with a thin layer of vermiculite, then wet with a misting bottle just to moisten the soil.
- Cover the flat with a plastic dome to create a humid environment and place in a warm location.
- Use grow lights to encourage germination and growth.
- Tag each flat with variety and date planted.
- Check flats twice daily, morning and night. Do not allow the seedling mix to dry out, but don't overwater.
- As soon as the seedlings begin to emerge, move the flat to a cooler (but not cold) location.
- When the second set of leaves emerges, begin applying diluted plant-starter fertilizer (e.g., 10-52-10 at quarter strength).

What are grow lights? Do I need them and why?

Lois ❖ Unless you're gardening on a large scale, you might find that the sun is the only grow light you need! In fact, when I first started in the greenhouse business, I never used grow lights. I just placed my seedling flats near a big, south-facing window. Over the years, I had good success—most of the time! Of course, when you rely entirely on Mother Nature you can expect a few surprises!

Grow lights are light bulbs that have been specifically designed to help plants to grow better. In some situations, grow lights provide plants with their only source of light. If you're starting a lot of seedlings or don't have adequate indoor light, grow lights can be a good investment.

Jim ❖ Actually, any light bulb is a grow light, since all light sources provide energy for plant growth. However, not all lights are created equal!

Standard incandescent bulbs (the type typically used in lamps around your home) emit too much infrared light (heat). Your seedlings end up overheating, and don't get enough of the visible light spectrum they need to grow well. Fluorescent lights are low in infrared light, so you can place them close to your seedlings. They don't produce quite as wide a light spectrum as commercial grow lights, but they do the job just fine.

In our greenhouses we use HID (High-Intensity Discharge) lights. Next to the sun itself, these are the ultimate grow lights—in fact, you can use them to grow tomatoes without any other source of light. However, HID lights can cost hundreds of dollars for a single fixture and the electrical bill can be staggering—a bit rich for the typical gardener!

A bright sunny window remains your least expensive option. If you're just starting a flat or two of seedlings, it will provide all the light you need.

'Tarmagon,' 'Walla Walla' & 'Lucifer' onions

Grow Light Pros and Cons

Regular incandescent
Pros
- Low initial cost, readily available

Cons
- Inefficient and more costly to run
- Heat may damage plants
- Narrow light spectrum (plants get far too much red light)

Regular fluorescent
Pros
- Moderate initial cost, ready availability
- Cool (may be placed close to plants)
- Much more efficient than incandescent
- Provide more "blue" light

Cons
- Do not provide adequate red light (which plants also need)
- Higher initial cost for fixtures and bulbs
- Produce far too little light energy for larger plants

Sunlight
Pros
- It's free!

Cons
- We can't control where and when (or even if!) the sun will shine

Consumer grow light
Pros
- Provides a balanced spectrum of "blue" and "red" light, while consuming nearly the same amount of electricity as traditional fluorescent lights.

Cons
- More expensive than regular fluorescent lights

HID lights
Pros
- Provide full spectrum of light needed for plant growth

Cons
- Very high initial cost and may provide too much light energy for young seedlings
- The overall colour band is yellow or silver gray, making the plants appear less attractive to the human eye

Is my windowsill too cold for starting seedlings in the winter?

Lois ❖ Windowsills are both good and bad. During the day they allow lots of sunlight in to encourage healthy growth on vegetable seedlings. On the other hand, the direct sunlight can cause seedlings to overheat and stretch. Cool air can spill down windows at night, chilling the seedling flats.

Jim ❖ Seedling flats need consistently warm, moist soil until the seedlings emerge. Then they need to be cooled to around 16–18°C for warm-season crops and 12–16°C for cool-season crops. The windowsill is often either too hot or too cold. Ideally, you should keep your seedlings in a bright, relatively cool environment until you transplant them. Half a metre away from the sill is better than right at the window.

How should I water my seedlings?

Lois ❖ Always wet the seedling soil prior to sowing. Thereafter, use a very fine, specially designed seedling nozzle to prevent washing out the seed or damaging the seedlings. You can also use a good misting bottle to keep the soil moist until the seedlings emerge.

Jim ❖ Once you have thoroughly wetted the seedling mixture, your future waterings should simply replace the moisture that has been lost. Never saturate the mix. Oxygen is just as important to germination as moisture is.

My seedlings tend to become leggy. Some of them even flop over. What causes this?

Lois ❖ Leggy seedlings are always caused by high temperature, low light, or a combination of the two.

Jim ❖ I have two rules for avoiding legginess. First, grow warm until seedlings emerge, then cool down temperatures immediately. Second, grow seedlings in the brightest light possible, without letting them overheat.

Can I collect seeds from hybrid plants and plant them next year?

Lois ❖ No, the results are likely to be disappointing.

Jim ❖ You can collect and sow hybrid seeds, but only half of the resulting plants will look like the variety that you collected the seed from. The other half will be divided evenly—the two quarters resembling the two parents that gave rise to the hybrid.

What is an inoculant? When should I use it?

Lois ❖ An inoculant is a powder used on peas and beans to help them extract nutrients from the soil. You apply it to your seeds just before you plant them.

Jim ❖ Inoculant contains bacterial soil micro-organisms. The nitrogen-fixing bacteria *Rhizobia* are the one of most common inoculants. *Rhizobia* infect the roots of peas and beans, then convert nitrogen gas in the soil into a useable form for the plant.

Use only fresh inoculant mixture; otherwise, most of the bacteria may be dead. Inoculant usually comes in a small plastic bag and looks like black powder. The simplest way to apply inoculant is to pour a bit of it into a packet of seeds, give the packet a good shake, and then sow the seeds.

What is damping off? Can I prevent it?

Lois ❖ Damping off is a group of fungal diseases that cause seedlings to rot. You can buy treated seed, which is lightly coated with a fungicide to protect seeds and seedlings from "damping off" or rotting.

Jim ❖ The best prevention is four-fold:

- Use a good-quality pasteurized *soilless* seedling mix. Most organisms that cause damping off are found in soil.

- Germinate seedlings in good light.

- Keep the soil moist but not wet. Never overwater. A damping-off organism called *Pythium* thrives in wet soil.

- Leave adequate space between seedlings. Crowded seedlings compete with each other for light and become stretched, which makes them more susceptible to diseases such as damping off.

I've heard Lois say to always plant thickly. Does this apply to seedlings as well?

Lois ❖ No! It's far better to seed thinly in the seedling flats. Otherwise, you'll end up with weak and spindly seedlings, because they're forced to compete for light. You'll also have a lot more trouble transplanting because it's so hard to separate the closely packed seedlings.

Jim ❖ Densely planted seedlings become spindly and weak very quickly, and they are much more vulnerable to a number of fungal diseases— diseases that lead to damping off. Thick, stocky stems are much less prone to infection.

Can I buy seed for all the vegetables sold in the greenhouse?

Lois ❖ Most seeds are available to home gardeners. However, some commercial seed breeders choose not to sell their seeds directly to the consumer, for one reason or another. For example, new varieties may not be available to the retail consumer until a few years after they are released because there is only enough seed available to supply commercial growers.

Jim ❖ Some seeds cost more because of the expensive breeding work required to produce new varieties—hybrids fall into this category. The labour to manage these crops, harvesting in particular, can be tedious and costly. As a result, some seed companies tend to sell the harvested seed only to commercial growers for the first few years. Customers as a rule would not be prepared to pay the high price for this seed, so making it available to home gardeners is simply not profitable.

'Cumberland' cauliflower

Expected viability of stored seed

1 year
onion, parsnip

2 years
leek, corn, okra, pepper

3 years
asparagus, bean, kohlrabi, broccoli, carrots, celeriac, Chinese cabbage, pea, spinach

4 years
beet, Brussels sprouts, cabbage, cauliflower, eggplant, fennel, kale, pumpkin, rutabaga, squash, Swiss chard, tomato, turnip

5 years
cucumber, endive, radish

6 years
lettuce

Do seeds carry diseases?

Lois ❖ Unfortunately, yes. On the bright side, however, thanks to current technology today's seeds harbour far fewer seed-borne diseases than their predecessors.

Jim ❖ Seeds can carry many different diseases, including viruses, bacteria, and fungi. However, seed companies spend a great deal of time and effort eliminating many diseases long before the seed is packaged and sold. By far the greatest disease problems exist on seeds collected from home gardens. I'm not saying that you shouldn't keep collecting your seeds—just be aware that the risk of seed-borne disease is greater.

Do seeds keep indefinitely? How should I store them?

Lois ❖ Some seeds last longer than others, but none will last indefinitely.

Jim ❖ The better the storage conditions, the longer the period that seeds can be stored viably.

What exactly is an organic seed?

Jim ❖ Organic seed is seed grown from plants that have grown without synthetic pesticides or commercially synthesized fertilizers. Organic seed has also not been treated with any of these products after harvest.

I want to save seed from my vegetables. How do I collect seed?

Jim ❖ It varies. Some plants, such as potatoes and sweet potatoes, are not grown from seeds but from tubers. Some plants are hybrids and will not grow true to type if you plant the collected seed. Non-hybrid peas, squash and beans will produced viable seeds, provided you give them time to ripen fully. Seed will not mature after it has been harvested: it must mature fully on the plant.

Remember that some vegetables, such as carrots, cabbage, and cauliflower, are biennial, meaning that they don't produce seed until the second year. In other words, in our climate at least, you'll have to make do with store-bought seeds!

Will vegetables reseed themselves?

Lois ❖ Some will, some won't. Pumpkins and squash self-sow, or "volunteer," readily, as do spinach, peas, and lettuce.

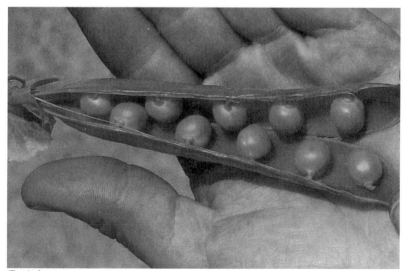

'Patriot' peas

Transplanting

Lois, you've always said, "Plant early!" Isn't this risky in a cold country like Canada?

Lois ❖ Not at all! Many people wait far too long to plant, under the mistaken impression that even a touch of frost will wipe out all of their vegetables. But a vast number of vegetables are very frost tolerant.

Another benefit of seeding early is that the moisture level in your garden is higher, which means better conditions for germinating seedlings.

Jim ❖ Not only does planting early offer earlier yields, but many vegetables actually benefit because they prefer to grow in the spring, before the heat of midsummer. And in cool, short-season climates, some vegetables like corn must be started early for them to mature before fall frost. See the chart at left for more information—most commercial growers adhere to this schedule.

Are there any disadvantages to planting early?

Lois ❖ I have to admit, there are a couple. For example, the seed of warm-season vegetables can rot if sown into cold soil. I've never had success sowing heat-loving crops like cucumbers and squash when the soil is cold. People who wait until later in the season can also eliminate many of their weeds before planting. When you cultivate your garden after the first flush of weed seedlings, you can destroy the weeds that sprouted in the early spring. Those who plant early have to remove those weeds by hand from between their vegetables.

Of course, there's another way of looking at it. Weeds don't wait around until the end of May before getting busy in your garden, so why should you?

Frost tolerance of seedlings

Be sure to confirm the average date of the last spring frost for your area before planting.

Hardy Vegetables
(plant up to 5 weeks before date of average last spring frost)

asparagus, beet, broccoli, Brussels sprouts, cabbage, carrots, cauliflower, celeriac, celery, garlic, kale, kohlrabi, leek, lettuce, onion, parsnip, pea, potato, radish, rutabaga, spinach, Swiss chard, turnip

Tender Vegetables
(plant on or just before date of average last spring frost)

beans, corn, zucchini

Heat-loving Vegetables
(plant 1 or 2 weeks after the date of average last spring frost)

These vegetables (except cucumber and squash) should be transplanted into the garden rather than seeded.

cucumbers, eggplant, pepper, pumpkin, squash, tomato

Jim ❖ If you want to plant warm-season crops early, use fungicide-treated seed to reduce rot. Treated seeds are often coated with a pink dye, which identifies the seed as treated. Thiram is the fungicide used most often on treated seeds, because it is effective against many soil-borne, seed-rotting diseases.

Once your warm-season crops sprout, keep an eye on the weather forecast and simply cover them if there's a threat of frost.

Do I have to harden off my purchased vegetables or only the ones I grow myself?

Lois ❖ Most commercially grown transplants have already been hardened off by the greenhouse. You should be able to take them home and plant them right away. Transplants that haven't been properly hardened off can be easily injured by wind, sun, insects, disease, and sudden temperature drops.

Jim ❖ Hardening off involves gradually cooling the seedlings to a safe temperature level. I like to cool warm-season crops down to 16-18°C for a week and cool-season crops down to 12-14°C for the same length of time.

Mom's right, though. Most vegetable transplants you purchase are ready to go into the ground.

The roots of my vegetables have grown through the bottom of the plastic pack. Will I damage the plants when I transplant them?

Lois ❖ No, you won't hurt plants if you break off a few lower roots. In fact, it is advantageous to pull apart the roots once you have removed them from the pack to encourage them to spread into the garden soil. This is particularly important if the plants are becoming rootbound—that is, if the roots are all tangled and knotted together.

Jim ❖ Pulling the roots apart won't help for some rootbound transplants. Cabbage, cauliflower and corn shift into their reproductive phase once they become rootbound. Once this phase is initiated, it can't be stopped. As a result, the plants will remain stunted. For example, cauliflower and broccoli will "button," forming many tiny heads instead of one big, tasty head. Cucumbers, pumpkins, melons, and squash transplants don't like having their roots disturbed—or being pulled apart.

My plants are all stretched out in the packs. Should I cut them back before I transplant?

Lois ❖ No! You'll destroy most vegetable plants if you cut them back. You can trim lettuce and onions, but it is best to simply avoid purchasing stretched plants. Get to your greenhouse early in the season and buy stocky, robust transplants!

Jim ❖ You can't cut back most young vegetable plants because you would end up removing the growing point (the spot where all new growth is produced). One snip and the plant will simply cease to grow.

Young tomato plants do have several growing points. Even so, you'll set them back substantially if you cut them. Don't do it! You're better off trench-planting a lanky tomato plant (see page 133).

I kept my transplants in my garage, and they've started to turn yellow. Have I done something wrong?

Lois ❖ I call this "garage-plant syndrome." Don't leave your plants in the garage! Put them into the ground as soon as you have the chance. If necessary, postpone shopping for vegetable transplants until you have time to plant them.

That said, if you can't plant them right away, make sure to put them outside during the day, and only put them back in the garage at night if outside temperatures are expected to drop below freezing. Inside a garage, even near a window, plants don't receive nearly enough light to maintain healthy growth.

Jim ❖ Outside, even on a cloudy day, your plants receive at least twice as much light as they do indoors in front of a bright, south-facing window. At the same time, the outdoor conditions help prepare plants for transplanting. Keeping your plants out of the garage is just as important as keeping your car out of the garden!

What is the best fertilizer to use when transplanting plants?

Lois ❖ I've always used 10-52-10 plant starter fertilizer once per week for three weeks after transplanting.

Jim ❖ 10-52-10 is a good initial choice. The middle number indicates a high level of phosphorus, which is a major component of the plant's energy system and important to developing a healthy root system. But after about three weeks, it's time to shift to a more balanced, all-purpose fertilizer, such as 20-20-20.

That said, there really is no single "best" fertilizer for gardens, because soil fertility varies so much from yard to yard. I've seen both ends of the spectrum—from incredibly fertile to desperately barren. Some soils are so depleted of nutrients that they need large doses of "complete" fertilizers to rejuvenate them. Other soils are so rich in nutrients that they require no extra fertilizer at all. Only a soil test can determine exactly what nutrients a soil needs.

My cucumber packs have several plants growing in some of the cells. Should I plant them in a clump or separate them?

Lois ❖ Some vegetable transplants—cucumbers, melons, and pumpkins, for example—sometimes contain multiple seedlings per cell. Growers often place two or three seeds in each cell to ensure that at least one germinates. Plant the entire cell in the ground; you'll damage the seedlings if you try to separate them.

Jim ❖ With the exception of the crops Mom mentions above, don't deliberately purchase packs with extra seedlings. If you split the plants, you'll likely set them back considerably. As a result, these plants are no bargain!

What can I plant with onions to help them grow?

Lois ❖ Onions do very well all by themselves. In fact, they don't compete well with other plants, so I'm always careful to give onions their own place in the sun.

Jim ❖ In my opinion, companion planting has not proven to be effective. Plants compete for light, moisture, and nutrients. Companion planting creates a highly competitive environment; giving vegetables space does the most good. If you're having trouble with your onion patch, try adding lots of organic matter to the soil. Onions often have a difficult time pushing through soils with hard crusts, but they grow well from transplants.

'Kelsea Giant' onions

'Small Miracle' broccoli

Are there some vegetables that you should not plant together?

Lois ❖ Not particularly, provided you give all of your vegetables adequate room. Consider the mature size of each vegetable when you plant, so they won't end up having to compete for resources. For example, if you plant onions next to pumpkins, they'll be choked out as the pumpkin vines spread. And taller crops like corn can shade other, smaller vegetables.

Jim ❖ Most vegetables have negligible effects on one another. However, some plants exude chemicals that can injure other plants, a phenomenon called *allelopathy*. For example, cabbage, cauliflower and broccoli are members of the family Cruciferae. Once broken down in the soil, they release compounds, called glucosinolates, that may inhibit germination of some seedlings. It's not a huge concern, however.

Certain vegetables attract pests that then attack other plants. For example, planting potatoes near eggplant can attract Colorado potato beetles to the eggplant. Taking advantage of this notion of redirection, there are now "trap" plants on the market, like the 'Allure' tomato, which attracts potato beetles to itself and away from potatoes. This may sound great in theory, but I'm not convinced that it is effective in real-life garden situations.

The main consideration is giving each plant enough space, as Mom says. If you're uncertain how much space to allow, check the information on the seed packet or consult a reliable gardening book.

CHAPTER 4 ❧
THE GROWING SEASON

Nurturing a vegetable garden is a reward in itself. If you grow vegetables in containers, remember that, because of the limited soil volume, you need to check the pot every single day for moisture. Plan on watering containerized vegetables daily during hot spells, and be generous, especially with thirsty plants like tomatoes.

Spring

How should I prepare my vegetable garden in the spring?

Jim ❖ Here's a spring checklist for your vegetable garden:

- Cut down and compost or till in any remaining vegetation from the previous year. (It's actually easier to do this in the fall.)
- Add compost or well-rotted manure.
- Work the soil to create a smooth, lump-free seedbed. A rototiller can make this job easier, but don't overdo it!
- Control perennial weeds like thistle and quackgrass before planting. This may delay sowing and transplanting for several weeks until the weeds are under control. You can spray with glyphosate or undertake hoeing and tilling.

Watering

How often should I water my garden?

Lois ❖ It varies depending on the weather and the crop. Most varieties flourish with weekly waterings. Plants grown in containers require more water than established plants in the garden; check them every day.

Jim ❖ Water new transplants every couple of days until they're well established. After that, a thorough soaking once a week is usually sufficient. During extended hot, dry spells you may need to water every three or four days.

What's the best way to water my plants?

Lois ❖ I like to use a water wand with a good flood nozzle. It allows me to deliver the water right to the base of the plant, where it belongs. When watering, be sure to soak the soil thoroughly.

Jim ❖ The biggest mistake that many gardeners make when watering is to sprinkle the leaves instead of soaking the plant's base. When you water thoroughly, you encourage plants to develop deep root systems, allowing them to better tolerate dry spells.

Use a flood nozzle and water around the base of each plant. Try not to soak the foliage in the late evening, or you may promote diseases like grey mould and powdery mildew.

Can I use my sprinkler system on my vegetable garden?

Lois ❖ Yes. I used one for years with excellent results. Anyone who grows vegetables commercially usually has some sort of irrigation system. But remember that hand-watering is essential at times, no matter which system you have in the garden.

How much water does my garden need?

Jim ❖ As a general rule, your garden needs 2.5 cm of water per week. Take into account the amount of rainfall each week and subtract this from 2.5 cm. During wet weather your garden may require no extra watering. Other times, you may have to apply the full dose yourself. If you use a sprinkler, put tuna tins on the soil and turn off the sprinkler once they're full.

Try to avoid watering on hot, dry, windy days: you'll lose a lot of moisture to evaporation. Fine sprays of water evaporate much more quickly than coarse droplets, so don't use misting nozzles.

How can I tell if I'm overwatering?

Lois ❖ If all of a plant's leaves begin to turn yellow and the soil around it feels very wet, chances are it's waterlogged. Check your soil for proper drainage, add amendments if necessary (see Soil, chapter 1), and allow the soil surface to dry out between waterings.

It is rare to lose plants from overwatering. In my experience, this problems usually happens to vegetables grown in containers without drainage holes. What seems like overwatering generally reflects poorly drained, water-logged soil.

I can't keep my garden moist enough. What should I do?

Jim ❖ One option, if you have a large garden, is to install a drip-irrigation system and timers. You can also spread mulch in the garden to reduce water loss due to evaporation. You might also want to check whether your soil is overly porous; if it is, you can amend it to improve water retention.

Finally, examine your watering habits. Are you watering deeply and regu-larly, or does the garden get only occasional light sprinklings? Are you watering the leaves or the plant bases? Thorough watering encourages plants to develop deeper, stronger roots, which helps the plant to find water even when the soil surface is dry.

'Savoy Express' cabbage

Why are my plants still wilted when I have just watered them?

Jim ❖ Several factors can prevent plants from absorbing water properly. On a very hot day, a recently transplanted seedling may transpire moisture more quickly than it can draw it from the soil. Water on the foliage can temporarily bend the leaves down, but they will rebound once they are dry. Other problems, for example, root rot, also reduce your plant's ability to draw up moisture.

I've heard that I should be careful when watering on sunny days because water on the leaves can cause burning. Is this true?

Lois ❖ There's no truth at all to this popular myth. Water on leaves can, however, foster various diseases. Grey mould, for example, thrives on the moist foliage of susceptible plants like string beans. This is why I always recommend watering with a good flood nozzle, so that you can send all of the water to the soil around the base of the plant where it's needed.

Jim ❖ This myth simply refuses to die! Don't believe it! Look at it this way: what would happen if water droplets really did burn leaves? A brief rainstorm followed by sunshine would burn every plant for miles around!

That said, the only problem with watering during the heat of the day is some extra moisture loss due to evaporation. Water your garden first thing in the morning, to give your soil a chance to absorb as much of the water as possible.

My rain barrel is rusty. Could this cause problems for my plants?

Jim ❖ Possibly. The water might contain too much iron. Although iron is an essential plant nutrient, too much can lead to plant injury.

Fertilizer

On fertilizer packages, what do the three numbers represent?

Jim ❖ The numbers refer to the percentage by weight of nitrogen (the first number), phosphate (the middle number), and potash (the last number) in the fertilizer. Nitrogen is crucial for leaf growth, phosphates promote strong root development, and potash aids in all-around plant health.

Which fertilizer should I use?

Lois ❖ Fertilize new transplants once a week for three weeks with starter fertilizer (10-52-10), to promote vigorous roots and help your plants get established. After two or three weeks, switch to a good all-purpose (20-20-20) fertilizer once a month.

Jim ❖ Some gardeners rely almost entirely on compost and well-rotted manure, while others use granular or water-soluble fertilizers. I prefer 20-20-20 or 15-15-30 once a week during the spring and summer. For container vegetables, use a slow-release fertilizer like Smartcote 14-14-14.

Do brand names matter or is one 20-20-20 fertilizer like the next?

Jim ❖ The numbers represent a minimum chemical analysis; no reputable company would try to shortchange you. The only differences might be the ease with which the fertilizer dissolves, the chemical formulation of each nutrient, and the composition of the inert ingredients. In general, though, you'll find that most 20-20-20 fertilizers work well in your garden.

Salt tolerance of vegetables

Highly Sensitive Crops
bean
carrots
onion

Moderately Sensitive Crops
bean, broad
broccoli
cabbage
celery
corn
cucumber
lettuce
pepper
potato
radish
spinach
sweet potato
tomato
turnip

Moderately Tolerant Crops
beet
zucchini

How often should I fertilize my vegetables?

Lois ❖ It depends on the type of crop, the fertility of your soil, and the method you prefer. A green onion, being rather tiny, requires far less fertilizer than a large, vigorous plant like corn. Soils rich in organic matter need much less fertilizer than poor clay soils.

Some gardeners prefer to get all of their fertilizing over with in the spring by incorporating granular fertilizers into the soil. Others prefer to use water-soluble fertilizers throughout the season. Both methods produce excellent results, and I often combine them in my garden.

Is it possible to over-fertilize? How can I tell I've done it?

Jim ❖ Over-fertilizing is certainly possible—in fact, it's a common problem. People often apply too much fertilizer or too much of one nutrient (nitrogen, phosphorus, or potassium). Too much fertilizer can raise the salt levels in the soil and burn the roots and, subsequently, the leaves. Over-fertilizing elevates soil salt levels to a point at which the roots are unable to absorb water. This is one reason why over-fertilized plants appear burned: they are dehydrated.

Applying too much of one nutrient causes a different kind of problem. Too much nitrogen, for example, causes excessive leafy growth at the expense of tuber or fruit production.

'Spear It' cucumbers

Will I hurt my plants if I continue to use 10-52-10 after 3 weeks?

Lois ❖ No, but they'll grow better if you switch over to a good all-purpose fertilizer.

Jim ❖ You'll have smaller yields if you stay with 10-52-10 throughout the growing season. It won't provide enough nitrogen or potassium for your plants. As the season progresses and the plants get larger, they develop a greater demand for nitrogen and potassium. Potassium—represented by the third number on the fertilizer label—is particularly important when the plants begin to fruit.

Which works better, chemical or organic fertilizer?

Lois ❖ Both work equally well. As long as your plants get the nutrients they need, they don't really care about the source. I like to use water-soluble fertilizers because they act so quickly and are so easy to use, but many people achieve excellent results with fish fertilizers, kelp meal, manure teas, and even bat guano.

Jim ❖ All fertilizers are actually "chemical" fertilizers, in that they deliver the same elements and compounds to your plants. However, organic and non-organic fertilizers differ in the way they deliver these nutrients.

When you add manure to your soil, for example, micro-organisms in the soil digest it, breaking it down into separate compounds such as ammonium, nitrates, phosphates, and iron oxides. Chemical fertilizers, such as 20-20-20, also contain ammonium, iron, phosphates, and so on. Unlike organic fertilizers, however, they don't have to be broken down before releasing nutrients to the plant. In either case, the plant eventually absorbs the same compounds in the same form, whether it's from an organic or non-organic source.

Organic fertilizers generally have a low analysis (e.g., fish fertilizer is approximately 3-1-1), so you often need larger quantities to provide the same amount of nutrients as a chemical fertilizer. Keep in mind, however, that organic fertilizers provide more than short-term benefits to your plants. Because they take time to break down, they provide a long-term reservoir of nutrients in your soil. Manure, compost, and peat moss also improve your soil's texture and moisture retention.

Should I dilute fertilizer?

Lois ❖ It depends on the type of fertilizer. You must dilute most liquid fertilizers. Water-soluble fertilizers, of course, should be mixed with water before being applied. Granular fertilizers, on the other hand, are intended to be applied directly to the soil.

Jim ❖ If the fertilizer is too strong, it can burn plants. Always follow the directions on the label when mixing or applying fertilizer.

Why won't my granular fertilizer dissolve?

Jim ❖ Granular fertilizers are designed to be applied directly to the soil, where they slowly dissolve. Many of them aren't formulated to dissolve readily in water. Some will dissolve readily in water, even though they aren't intended as water-soluble fertilizers (34-0-0 for example). Others, like 11-51-0, contain many water-insoluble compounds (phosphates, calcium, etc) so they will not dissolve readily.

If you want to dissolve your fertilizer in water, simply choose a water-soluble fertilizer.

My plants need oxygen. Can I get liquid fertilizer with oxygen?

Jim ❖ Some fertilizers have been treated with peroxides that break down into oxygen. The theory is that plants will use this oxygen readily. Although this is partially true, no fertilizer on its own can provide enough oxygen to sustain plant growth.

The availability of oxygen for plant roots depends on soil texture. If a soil is "open" and has lots of pore spaces, the oxygen will easily move from the soil surface down to the roots. If the soil is compacted, no amount of oxygen-containing fertilizer will help. If lack of oxygen is a concern, spend your money on improving your soil texture instead.

Can I grow vegetables organically?

Lois ❖ It is certainly possible to grow good vegetables without synthetic fertilizers and insecticides. For years we grew most of our vegetables without any fertilizer or pesticides at all. We were fortunate to have lots of very rich, deep loam soil and only small numbers of insect and disease pests.

However, if you do garden organically, you must be prepared to accept a few more blemishes on the vegetables and even the occasional bug in your salad.

'Favor' carrots

What is manure tea?

Lois ❖ I've never made manure tea, or compost tea, but a lot of people swear by it. Like the name suggests, it's a liquid fertilizer made by soaking manure or compost in water.

You brew it in much the same way as you would Orange Pekoe, but in a bigger pot! Just shovel some manure or compost into a burlap bag and tie it shut. Then immerse your "tea bag" into a large bucket or barrel of water, cover it, and leave it to steep for a few days. Before using the liquid on your plants, be sure to dilute it to a very light brown.

Use the tea in place of regular water. In my opinion, the amount of work in brewing this tea far outweighs the benefit to the plants, but don't let me stop you from giving it a try.

Jim ❖ Keep a few points in mind when using manure or compost tea:

- Manure may contain plant diseases, and seedlings are especially susceptible.

- Manure teas may contain high levels of ammonia that can injure seedlings.

- Because tea is a weakened solution of manure, it may not contain enough nutrients for rapidly growing plants. As with any manure, the composition varies depending on the age and origin of the manure.

- Manure can contain disease organisms that may pose a human health risk.

Weeding

How can I minimize weeding?

Lois ❖ Minimize is the right word, because you'll never eliminate weeding entirely! Here are a few tips:

- Start off with a clean garden. Spend a full season if necessary to control weeds prior to planting, especially if perennial weeds like thistle and quackgrass are a major problem.
- Use only clean topsoil, compost, and manure.
- Never let annual weeds go to seed, and never put mature weeds into your compost.
- Eliminate perennial weeds before they have a chance to become established.
- Add mulch to your beds.
- Use a weed barrier where practical.

Should I use weed barrier in my vegetable beds?

Lois ❖ You can use weed-barrier cloth with vegetables that are widely spaced, such as tomatoes, peppers, eggplant, and squash. For other, more closely spaced crops, such as onions, lettuce, and carrots, scatter clean straw or other mulch around the base of the plants.

Jim ❖ If you decide to try a weed barrier, choose a high-quality black fabric: fewer weeds can grow through and it tends to be more durable. You must remember to soak your beds thoroughly when watering because the fabric intercepts some of the moisture.

What's the easiest way to pull weeds?

Lois ❖ If you weed a few days after a good rain, the weeds pull out of the soil more easily. It is much easier to weed after a rainfall than when the soil is very dry. If you do find yourself weeding a dry bed, use a sturdy hoe to get around the leaves of the weed, and pull it up from its base. I prefer a stirrup hoe: it's a very efficient tool! Be sure to add compost or peat moss to the garden every year to keep the soil soft and easy to weed.

Jim ❖ If you have a large garden, you may find it easier to control weeds by allowing enough space between the rows for a rototiller to pass, then hand weeding within the rows.

How do I get rid of weed seeds in my soil?

Lois ❖ Always, always try to plant into clean soil, and never allow the weeds in your garden to go to seed. It's worth the effort!

To eliminate a severe weed problem from your garden, keep it bare all summer. Rototill, hoe, or spray for weeds when necessary. Be very careful not to allow any weeds to go to seed. It's hard work, but it's the only way you'll be able to reduce your weed problem in the long run.

If you insist on planting a garden, try dividing your problem area in half. Plant one half of your garden, and treat the other half for weeds. Next year, switch sides—think of it like summer fallow.

Jim ❖ Here are my best tips for reducing your weed problem.

- Never allow the weeds to go to seed. A single pigweed can produce up to one million seeds each year!

- Perennial weeds that spread by rhizomes, such as quackgrass, require a rigorous, regular tillage program. You may have to till the soil weekly for an entire year to get rid of these persistent weeds. The best solution is to apply the herbicide glyphosate when the perennial weeds are 15–20 cm tall.

- Don't introduce weeds into your garden in the first place—always buy clean potting or garden soils.

- Never plant into areas infested with tough-to-control weeds like thistle or quackgrass: eliminate these weeds first.

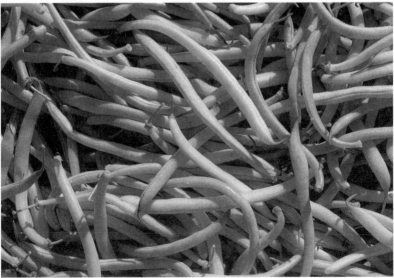

'Rocdor' beans

Container Growing

Can I grow vegetables in a pot on my deck or balcony?

Lois ❖ Absolutely. A determined gardener can always find a place to grow vegetables!

Tomatoes and peppers are the most common choices, but you can grow virtually any vegetable in containers (with the exception of really big ones, like Atlantic Giant pumpkins). I've even grown corn in big oak whisky barrels.

Jim ❖ Container growing gives you the advantage of starting with clean, soilless mixtures. You end up with cleaner vegetables and fewer pest and disease problems. Weeding is easy, too. On the other hand, vegetables in containers require more frequent watering and fertilizing, and you need to invest in pots and good-quality potting soil.

That said, growing in containers is a great idea for all gardeners, not just apartment and condo dwellers. Containers allow you to take advantage of light and heat as it changes through the growing season, and a bushy bean or vigorous tomato makes an attractive addition to the patio. I know one gardener who plants his tomatoes in containers set on wheeled trolleys. This way, he can move the plants around his deck and take advantage of the sun.

How big should my containers be?

Lois ❖ A 20-litre container will satisfy the needs of virtually all vegetables. You can use containers half this size for smaller crops like lettuce, radishes, and green onions.

Jim ❖ Make sure your containers have adequate root space, that they are large and heavy enough to stay in place in the wind, that they can hold enough water to sustain the plants, and that they're deep enough to permit root crops to develop to their full potential.

Can I grow vegetables in a sunroom?

Lois ❖ Small, leafy, shade-tolerant vegetables can do reasonably well in a sunroom. Larger vegetables will tend to languish, unless the room is exceptionally bright, like a greenhouse.

Jim ❖ Vegetables need a lot of light. Some vegetables have a hard time capturing enough sunlight outdoors, let alone indoors. Even a sunroom can have insufficient light, particularly in the winter when the sun is low and the days are short. You need to supplement the light with high-intensity grow lights, which are expensive and often impractical.

Even that might not be enough. Some crops—squash, pumpkins and field cucumbers, for example—need bees for pollination, and a huge amount of space to grow. These vegetables will not grow well in a sunroom.

Can I grow a pepper inside my house?

Lois ❖ No. The plant will not receive enough light and will probably die. You certainly won't get any peppers!

Jim ❖ People harvest plants, but plants harvest light. If they don't get enough light, they simply won't produce fruit.

You might think that a bright, sunny location near a window would provide adequate light for a pepper plant, but it's far from sufficient. The situation is even worse during winter, with its low light intensity and short days.

If I grow peppers in my greenhouse, do I have to pollinate them by hand?

Lois ❖ Peppers are almost entirely self-pollinated and don't require hand pollination. They will produce fruit without any help.

Jim ❖ Self-pollinating plants produce flowers that can pollinate themselves. The pollen doesn't have to be passed from one flower to another.

Tomatoes also self-pollinate, but when you grow them in a greenhouse it's helpful to shake the flower clusters with, say, an electric toothbrush. When you do this you'll end up with a higher yield and better-quality tomatoes. But remember to pollinate at midday, when the flowers are most receptive to pollination.

Days from pollination to harvest under warm conditions

Vegetable	Days
bean	7–10
corn	18–23
cucumber, pickling	4–5
cucumber, slicing	15–18
eggplant	25–40
okra	4–6
pepper, green	45–55
pepper, red	60–70
pumpkin, early-season	65–75
squash, summer	4–7
squash, winter	55–90
tomato, red	45–60
zucchini	3–4

Can I grow potatoes in tires?

Lois ❖ You can grow potatoes in washing machines or old bathtubs if you like. But yes, I've heard of growing potatoes in tires, although it remains more of a novelty than a way of increasing potato yields.

People who do this plant the potato in a tire, and keep adding more straw or lightweight soil mixture as the plant grows. When it's time to harvest, they strip the tires off.

Jim ❖ Instead of growing in tires, I'd recommend a relatively new invention, the potato barrel. You fill the barrel with lightweight potting mix, then water and fertilize the potato plants regularly. The barrels have gates in the side that open up for easy harvesting. I find that potato barrels produce healthy, super-clean, delicious potatoes.

Do containers need extra water?

Lois ❖ Yes. Containerized plants need more water than those grown in the garden. Larger containers can hold more moisture than small containers, but you'll still need to water them almost every day.

Jim ❖ Yes, you should water containerized vegetables every day during hot, sunny weather. The same vegetables growing in the garden may need water only once a week.

In the garden, water moves greater distances both down into the soil and horizontally. This provides your plants with a much greater moisture reserve. At the same time, in the garden the roots of your plants have a lot more room to spread. A plant in a container is essentially a captive in a closed environment. You have to provide it with everything it needs—and that includes plenty of water.

How do I know whether I've watered my containers enough? Should water be dripping out of the bottom?

Lois ❖ You've got to thoroughly soak the container each and every time. Don't just "baptize" your plants! Sprinkling a bit of water on the surface results in shallow, under-developed roots. You want the moisture to go right to the bottom. I like to water until I see water flowing from the bottom of the pot.

Jim ❖ Water your containers every time the top couple of centimetres of soil surface begins to dry out. Assuming you have good potting soil, it's nearly impossible to overwater. Properly balanced soil retains the right amount of moisture, and allows any excess to drain away. If your soil doesn't stay moist or if it becomes waterlogged, you should choose better-quality potting soil.

Over the years, it has been customers who under-water garden plants that have experienced the most problems—rarely is overwatering by itself an issue.

Maintaining the Garden

If I cover my plants at night, won't the cover crush the plants?

Lois ❖ No, provided you use a lightweight fabric. Plants are stronger than you think, and the weight of fabric distributed over all the plants won't harm them. That's not to say that you should toss a heavy quilt over your tomatoes! Lightweight covers like burlap and bedsheets are a better choice. Avoid fabrics that can absorb lots of rain, since the weight of the water could cause the covers to crush the plants.

Jim ❖ Lightweight fabrics are best. You might even consider buying spun polyester fabrics like Remay cloth. They are very lightweight and provide several degrees of frost protection.

'Golden Girl' tomatoes

Can I cover my plants with sheets of plastic or plastic buckets? I don't want my good cotton sheets to get dirty.

Lois ❖ Chances are, your sheets won't get anything on them that doesn't come out in the wash. However, if you're worried about your good sheets, keep them out of the garden! Dig some old sheets out of the closet, or grab some towels or burlap sacking. Don't use plastic, though, because it provides no insulation. Most garden centres sell a frost blanket that is durable and easy to use, stores well and offers excellent protection to your plants.

Jim ❖ Plastic buckets provide some insulation, but they're not as effective as ordinary fabric. Plastic sheets provide no insulation at all. They're only useful if attached to the foundation of your house and draped over your plants. This traps some of the heat from your house. However, light fabric is still your simplest and most effective option.

Are there non-chemical products that I can garden with?

Jim ❖ No. All products used in the garden are chemicals. However, organic gardeners draw a line between naturally occurring pesticides and fertilizers and man-made pesticides and fertilizers. Each fertilizer or pesticide must be judged on its own merit, rather than categorizing whether or not it is "organic" or "synthetic."

Some of the most powerful poisons occur naturally, while some of the weakest are man-made. It's important to understand the products you intend to use in the garden. If you have any doubts, get advice from experts.

Is it beneficial to put broken eggshells around my tomato plants?

Lois ❖ I've always put broken eggshells around my plants.

Jim ❖ Eggshells do contain calcium, which is an essential plant nutrient. As they break down, they release it gradually into the soil. Don't expect them to perform miracles in the garden, however. Egg shells won't have a huge impact on the calcium levels in your soil, but neither will they do any harm. So by all means, sprinkle them around your tomato plants or add them to your compost.

'Space Miser' zucchini

Can I chop up my vegetable scraps and put them in my garden, or should I compost them first?

Lois ❖ I recommend that you compost them first. They don't look very nice if you throw them directly into the garden. The scraps will gradually break down on their own, releasing nutrients and improving the soil texture, but you're better off putting them into the composter first.

Jim ❖ Never throw diseased vegetation into the garden, whether the produce was purchased from a grocery or homegrown. The disease could infect healthy vegetables. Composting kills some disease organisms but not all of them.

I've heard about using the sun's angle to increase vegetable yields. How is this done?

Jim ❖ This is an old technique used in such diverse locales as England and southern California. The trick is to use the sun's angle to heat the soil and speed up the growth of vegetable crops. On a south-facing slope, the sun's rays hit the soil surface almost perpendicularly, increasing the amount of energy striking each square centimetre of soil.

The best slope is quite steep, which is impractical for many gardeners, but any south-facing slope will increase the overall energy received from the sun. For example, a bed sloped to 35 degrees to the south will absorb about 33 percent more solar energy than a flat plain of equal dimensions.

Getting Ready for Fall

How should I prepare my vegetable garden for the next growing season?

Lois ❖ Do as much as you can in the fall to reduce the work in the spring. Spring is busy enough as it is! Add lots of organic material to the soil and dig or rototill, leaving large lumps in the garden that will break down over the winter. Coarse lumps catch snow, which will add to the available moisture in your garden the following spring.

Jim ❖ Be sure to eliminate any disease-ridden foliage, to reduce hiding places for overwintering insects.

Should I just turn my dead plants under in the fall?

Lois ❖ You can do this, but be sure to remove any diseased vegetation to prevent diseases from carrying over to the next spring.

Jim ❖ The organic material from old vegetables is good for the garden, but Mom's right: if the vegetables had serious diseases during the growing season, you must remove them. And remember, never put diseased plants in your compost pile!

'Georgia Jet' sweet potato

CHAPTER 5 ❧
PRESERVING THE HARVEST

Ideal storage conditions are hard to provide in most homes. In most household storage situations, heat, cold, and humidity can be difficult to control. But this obstacle is far from insurmountable. You can use the fridge or the pantry as long as you don't expect your produce to last forever. And remember that no matter how ideal your storage conditions, vegetables will never improve in storage; at best, you can only delay their inevitable decline. But while they last, you'll want to enjoy them to the fullest.

Storage Basics

How do I prepare vegetables for storage?

Lois ❖ If you remember nothing else about vegetable storage, remember this: garbage in, garbage out. I've made the mistake of not being able to part with some poor-quality vegetables and placed them in storage with good ones. Not only did the poor vegetables rot, but they also took their compatriots with them. The lesson to be learned is never put questionable vegetables in storage.

Jim ❖ Even with high-quality vegetables, some preparation is necessary before storage. As Mom said, don't put poor-quality vegetables in storage. Inspect vegetables for soft spots, blemishes, and bruising. Remove the damage, if possible, and use them quickly. Some vegetables, like rutabaga, can be cut into pieces and stored in the fridge. Other vegetables, like onions, need to be dried and cured.

Remove the soil from the vegetables you store. Some vegetables, like potatoes, should never be washed before storage, while others, like carrots, need all the soil washed off thoroughly.

Which vegetables shouldn't I mix together in storage?

Lois ❖ First and foremost, vegetables must be stored with other vegetables that prefer the same temperature ranges and humidity. For example, carrots shouldn't be stored with squash because carrots like temperatures near freezing, while squash likes temperatures around 10°C. At 0°C, squash freezes and is irreparably damaged, while at 10°C, carrots have a much-reduced storage life. Squash needs dry storage, while carrots store best at very high humidity.

Jim ❖ Vegetables can be further divided into those that are ethylene sensitive and those that produce lots of ethylene. Ethylene, a naturally occuring gas, is produced by plants and acts as a hormone. Excessive levels of ethylene cause premature deterioration of some vegetables. Injured tissue also emits a considerable amount of ethylene. Apples are notorious for emitting high levels of ethylene, which can injure sensitive vegetables.

Properly prepare the planting area for your asparagus (see page 99).

Does storage affect nutritional quality?

Jim ❖ In most cases, storage has little effect on nutritional quality.

Composition of fresh raw vegetables
Values are per 100 g of edible vegetable.

Vegetable	Water (%)	Energy (Calories)	Protein (g)	Fat (g)	Carbohydrate (g)
artichoke	84	51	2.7	0.2	11.9
asparagus	92	22	3.1	0.2	3.7
bean, green	90	31	1.8	0.1	7.1
bean, lima	70	113	6.8	0.9	20.2
beet greens	92	19	1.8	0.1	4.0
beet roots	87	44	1.5	0.1	10.0
broccoli	91	28	3.0	0.4	5.2
Brussels sprouts	86	43	3.4	0.3	9.0
cabbage, Chinese	94	16	1.2	0.2	3.2
cabbage, common	93	24	1.2	0.2	5.4
carrots	88	43	1.0	0.2	10.1
cauliflower	92	24	2.0	0.2	4.9
celery	95	16	0.7	0.1	3.6
corn	76	86	3.2	1.2	19.0
cucumber	96	13	0.5	0.1	2.9
eggplant	92	26	1.1	0.1	6.3
endive	94	17	1.3	0.2	3.4
garlic	59	149	6.4	0.5	33.1
kale	85	50	3.3	0.7	10.0
kohlrabi	91	27	1.7	0.1	6.2
leek	83	61	1.5	0.3	14.1
lettuce, loose leaf	94	18	1.3	0.3	3.5
onion, bunching	92	25	1.7	0.1	5.6
onion, dry	91	34	1.2	0.3	7.3
parsnip	80	75	1.2	0.3	18.0
pea, edible pod	89	42	2.8	0.2	7.6
pea, green	79	81	5.4	0.4	14.5
pepper, hot	88	40	2.0	0.2	9.5
pepper, sweet	93	25	0.9	0.5	5.3
potato	79	79	2.1	0.1	18.0
pumpkin	92	26	1.0	0.1	6.5
radish	95	17	0.6	0.5	3.6
rutabaga	90	36	1.2	0.2	8.1
spinach	92	22	2.9	0.4	3.5
squash, summer	94	20	1.2	0.2	4.4
squash, winter	89	37	1.5	0.2	8.8
Swiss chard	93	19	1.8	0.2	3.7
tomato	94	19	0.9	0.2	4.3
turnip	92	27	0.9	0.1	6.2
zucchini	96	14	1.2	0.1	2.9

Fibre (g)	Calcium (mg)	Phosphorus (mg)	Sodium (mg)	Potassium (mg)
1.1	48	77	80	339
0.8	22	52	2	302
1.1	37	38	6	209
1.9	34	136	8	467
1.3	119	40	201	547
0.8	16	48	72	324
1.1	48	66	27	325
1.5	42	69	25	389
0.6	77	29	9	238
0.8	47	23	18	246
1.0	27	44	35	323
0.9	29	46	15	355
0.7	36	26	88	284
0.7	2	89	15	270
0.6	14	17	2	149
1.0	36	33	4	219
0.9	52	28	22	314
1.5	181	153	17	401
1.5	135	56	43	447
1.0	24	46	20	350
1.5	59	35	20	180
0.7	68	25	9	264
0.8	60	33	4	257
0.4	25	29	2	155
2.0	36	71	10	375
2.5	43	53	4	200
2.2	25	108	5	244
1.8	18	46	7	340
1.2	6	22	3	195
0.4	7	46	6	543
1.1	21	44	1	340
0.5	21	18	24	232
1.1	47	58	20	337
0.9	99	49	79	558
0.6	20	35	2	195
1.4	31	32	4	350
0.8	51	46	213	379
0.5	7	23	8	207
0.9	30	27	67	191
0.5	15	32	3	248

Vegetable injuries in cold storage conditions

Most Susceptible
asparagus
bean, snap
cucumber
eggplant
lettuce
okra
pepper, sweet
potato
squash, summer
sweet potato
tomato

Moderately Susceptible
broccoli
cabbage, new
carrots, topped
cauliflower
celery
onion, dry
pea
radish, topped
spinach
squash, winter

Least Susceptible
beet
Brussels sprouts
cabbage, old and savoy
kale
kohlrabi
parsnip
rutabaga
turnip, topped

Storage Temperature

Can I store vegetables in my refrigerator?

Lois ❖ Yes, but household fridges aren't as good as commercial vegetable coolers, so the duration of storage is shorter. However, I've kept carrots for 6 months without a problem. The trick is to clean the carrots very well before storage and keep them as cold as possible (0°C is best).

Jim ❖ Household fridges, although cold, aren't cold enough for long-term storage of many vegetables. Because there is little air exchange, harmful gasses (to vegetables, not people) like ethylene build up and can injure stored vegetables. The humidity is also very low in fridges, and vegetables tend to dehydrate after even a short time in the fridge.

'Golden Hubbard' squash

Vegetable storage life at optimum temperature and relative humidity

Vegetable	Temperature (°C)	Relative Humidity (%)	Storage Life
artichoke, globe	0	95–100	2–3 weeks
artichoke, Jerusalem	-1–0	90–95	4–5 months
asparagus	0–2	95–100	2–3 weeks
bean, lima	3–5	95	5–7 days
bean, snap	4–7	95	7–10 days
beet, topped	0	98–100	4–6 months
broccoli	0	95–100	10–14 days
Brussels sprouts	0	95–100	3–5 weeks
cabbage, Chinese	0	95–100	2–3 months
cabbage, early	0	98–100	3–6 weeks
cabbage, late	0	98–100	5–6 months
carrots, baby	0	98–100	4–6 weeks
carrots, mature	0	98–100	7–9 months
cauliflower	0	95–98	3–4 weeks
celeriac	0	97–99	6–8 months
celery	0	98–100	2–3 months
corn	0	95–98	5–8 days
cucumber	10–13	95	10–14 days
eggplant	8–12	90–95	1 week
endive	0	95–100	2–3 weeks
garlic	0	65–70	6–7 months
kale	0	95–100	2–3 weeks
kohlrabi	0	98–100	2–3 months
leek	0	95–100	2–3 months
lettuce	0	98–100	2–3 weeks
okra	7–10	90–95	7–10 days
onion, dry	0	65–70	1–8 months
onion, green	0	95–100	3–4 weeks
parsnip	0	98–100	4–6 months
pea	0	95–98	1–2 weeks
pepper, hot	0–11	60–70	6 months
pepper, sweet	7–13	90–95	2–3 weeks
potato, late	3–4	90–95	5–10 months
pumpkin	10–13	50–70	2–3 months
radish	0	95–100	3–4 weeks
rhubarb	0	95–100	2–4 weeks
rutabaga	0	98–100	4–6 months
spinach	0	95–100	10–14 days
squash, summer	5–10	95	1–2 weeks
squash, winter	10	50–70	varies
Swiss chard	0	95–100	10–14 days
tomato, ripe	8–10	90–95	4–7 days
turnip	0	95	4–5 months

Why do I have to store my vegetables so cold?

Jim ❖The reason most vegetables are stored cold is to slow down the rate at which they use up their energy reserves (respiration rate) and to reduce moisture loss. For every degree of temperature increase, respiration rate and moisture loss increase dramatically.

Lowest safe storage temperatures

Vegetable	Lowest Safe Temperature (°C)
asparagus	0–2
bean, lima	1–4
bean, snap	7
cucumber	7
eggplant	7
pepper, sweet	7
potato	3
pumpkin	10
squash, winter	10
sweet potato	13
tomato, ripe	7–10
tomato, mature green	13

Why is the speed of cooling so important?

Jim ❖ Once a vegetable is harvested, it quickly undergoes many biochemical changes, some of which have a negative affect on flavour. These changes are temperature-dependent: the warmer the temperature, the quicker the changes.

When vegetables are taken from a warm garden and placed in the fridge, the central core of the vegetable can take hours to cool. In the meantime, irreversible changes take place that affect flavour and storage life. The best way to avoid this problem is to cool the vegetables down as quickly as possible.

When we used to farm vegetables commercially, we would try to harvest early in the morning, before the heat of day. Corn harvested at noon on warm, sunny days held so much heat that if we placed our hands in the centre of the bin, the corncobs felt hot!

What is hydrocooling?

Lois ❖ Hydrocooling is a fancy name for a vegetable ice-bath. Vegetables are plunged into ice water to quickly cool them down to a low temperature so that they will last longer in storage.

Jim ❖ Chilled water removes heat from vegetables much more rapidly and completely than cool air. For many vegetables that are harvested in the heat of the day, this is critical to prevent deterioration.

For some vegetables it's more critical than for others. Corn is often hydrocooled because the sugars begin to be converted into starch the moment the corn is picked; the hotter the corn, the quicker the deterioration. Hydrocooling slows this conversion by cooling the cobs quickly. Hydrocooling works well on corn and a few other durable vegetables, but it is too rough on delicate vegetables like beans.

What is controlled-atmosphere storage?

Jim ❖ Controlled-atmosphere storage is used in some commercial storage operations. It is expensive and requires specialized equipment and training. The principle is to modify the air or atmosphere in the storage facility to extend the length of storage of certain vegetables while maintaining the highest quality. Research has shown that, for certain vegetables, increasing carbon dioxide and reducing oxygen increases storage life. Controlled atmosphere storage can't be done in home storage because of the cost and expertise required.

Storage Processes

What is curing?

Jim ❖ Curing is the process of heat-treating certain vegetables prior to storing. Heating removes moisture from the outer layers of vegetables like onions, thereby reducing the activity of disease organisms. Heat-treated onions also develop dried scales on the bulb surface that act as a moisture barrier, reducing moisture loss in storage. Cured onions can last for 9 months in storage. Curing temperatures for onions are typically mid to high 20s for a few days.

'Esmeralda' lettuce

Which vegetables freeze well?

Lois ❖ Many vegetables freeze well. My general rule is to choose vegetables that store poorly at temperatures above 0°C, such as peas, beans, and corn.

The key is to cool, clean, and blanch them as soon as possible after harvesting, and to freeze them as quickly as possible. Spread the vegetables in thin layers in freezer bags and distribute them around the freezer until they are completely frozen. Once they're solidly frozen, you can stack for more efficient storage.

Vegetables that freeze well

asparagus
beans, green or yellow
beans, lima or broad
broccoli
Brussels sprouts
carrots
cauliflower
corn
kohlrabi
onions
parsnips
peas
pumpkin
rutabaga
squash, winter or
    summer
turnip
zucchini

Is it safe to store vegetables in my garage?

Lois ❖ Absolutely. There are several factors to consider when you store your vegetables:

- Is the space heated? If the temperature in your garage drops below freezing, it is not suitable. On the other hand, if it's very warm, your vegetables will not last as long in storage.

- Is there a lot of light in the garage? Vegetables (especially potatoes) store poorly in light.

- Never store vegetables directly on a concrete floor. The vegetables will "sweat" at the point where they touch the floor, and rot. I put a layer of newspaper between the floor and my produce; clean wooden planks or shelves are also fine.

- Certain vegetables, such as carrots and cabbages, require more humidity than a garage can offer, so they do not store well there. Potatoes, onions, and winter squash generally keep well in the garage.

Storing Specific Vegetables

Cabbage

Why are my cabbage heads turning yellow inside the head in storage?

Jim ❖ Many vegetables are highly sensitive to a naturally occurring gas called ethylene. Ethylene gas is emitted by vegetables at rates that vary depending on the vegetable. Some vegetables give off relatively large quantities of ethylene, and some vegetables are very sensitive to excessive levels of ethylene. Cabbage responds to excess ethylene by turning yellow. Ethylene levels of only 1 part per million can cause this problem. Apples are notorious for producing lots of ethylene and should not be stored with vegetables.

Carrots

What is the best way to store carrots?

Lois ❖ I've had great success storing carrots in the crisper in any refrigerator, provided the carrots are thoroughly washed before going into the fridge. The carrots must be cold (don't put carrots that are warm from the field in the fridge) and they should be stored in perforated bags to let excess moisture out. I leave my carrots in the garden for as long as possible. This shortens the storage time required, if only by a few weeks. And by October, the soil is colder when I harvest, so the carrots keep longer.

Jim ❖ The rule is to keep the carrots clean, cold, and moist. Carrots with soil attached often harbour disease organisms that get a free ride to the storage area, so wash them thoroughly. A temperature close to 0°C degrees is ideal. High humidity (95 percent) is great for reducing moisture loss.

Can I store carrots in sand?

Lois ❖ Many people store carrots in clean, moist sand. Wash them thoroughly before storing and keep the sand as close to freezing as possible.

Jim ❖ Sand is an old method of storing that actually works quite well. The carrots don't get too dry or too moist, but the temperatures must be kept cold for best results.

Leeks

How do I store leeks?

Lois ❖ Leeks store reasonably well if kept cold and humid. Store them at the freezing mark with high humidity (95–100 percent). They will keep for months under these conditions.

Onions

How do I know when onions can be put into storage?

Lois ❖ When the necks of onions weaken and the tops topple over and dry, the onions can be lifted and either dried in the field (if the weather is sunny and warm and over 24°C) or cured in storage.

In my area, fall is often cool and wet, so I spread my onions on newspaper in a warm, sheltered area if they are not completely cured in the garden. Another trick is to put them into long chains by braiding the tops and hanging them in the garage (see below). This way the onions dry, get lots of air movement, and don't take up much space. When you need an onion, just cut it from the braid.

How do I make an onion rope?

Lois ❖ Onion ropes are a beautiful way to store onions! Making an onion rope is easy.

Take 75–80 cm of strong string (it must be able support about 10 kg of onions). Tie an onion to one end of the string, then tie the other end to a ceiling hook or other strong support. (The string should be hanging at a comfortable height in front of you.)

Join two onions by twisting their tops together. Put one onion on either side of the string, then twist the onions together with the string in two or three turns. Push the onions to rest on the bottom onion. Join another pair of onions, first by twisting their tops together then by twisting them with string. Push them down to the pair below, but offset them so that they form a criss-cross with the first pair.

Continue to twist together pairs of onions, offsetting them alternately as you push them down the string. When the string is full, tie a single knot at the top and hang the rope in a cool, dry, dark place.

Potatoes

How should I store my potatoes? I have a cold room with a wooden floor, but the wood has a funny odour. Should I set the potatoes on the floor or keep them off the floor?

Lois ❖ I've stored potatoes in piles on a wood floor for many year with excellent results. Just be sure that the slats are clean and dry.

Jim ❖ Cleanliness is absolutely critical for long-term storage of vegetables. Ensure that the surface you are storing on has been sanitized. Disease can carry over from one year to the next on wooden surfaces. Carefully remove all debris and bleach the surface to destroy bacteria and fungi.

The odd smell from the wood could be due to dampness and rot. Replace any rotting wood before storing your vegetables.

How do I keep my potatoes from going green in storage?

Lois ❖ Potatoes exposed to light respond by turning green. It doesn't take much light to cause greening: even incandescent lights can cause this problem. Don't eat green potatoes.

Jim ❖ Potatoes that are bruised, left out in the field after harvest, or peeking out of their hills can accumulate toxic chemicals called glycoalkaloids. Potato tubers containing these chemicals are rarely eaten in large numbers because they taste bitter, but just the same, green or damaged tubers should be avoided.

Why have my potatoes gone black in the centres in storage?

Jim ❖ Potatoes can develop a condition called blackheart from being stored at temperatures that are too warm (over 15°C) and under anaerobic conditions (low oxygen). This usually occurs deep in a pile of potatoes where there is very little air movement. It usually doesn't show up until late winter. The tubers are simply starved for oxygen, particularly at their centres, and the tissue dies and turns black.

Dark french fries are also the result of low oxygen and warm storage temperatures.

My potatoes taste sweet after storing them. Why?

Lois ❖ Potatoes that get chilled in storage develop an off flavour. I've had many potatoes develop this sickly sweet flavour from storing them at temperatures that were too cold.

Jim ❖ Chilled tubers develop high levels of reducing sugars and often have dark flesh. Don't let the temperatures drop lower than 5°C. This is rarely a problem in the home, but it may occur when potatoes are stored up against cold concrete walls and foundations.

Can I store potatoes touched by frost?

Lois ❖ Frozen potatoes are like apples: it only takes one bad one to spoil the bunch. If you have frozen potatoes, they will slowly but surely rot good potatoes in their vicinity. Just the smell of rotting potatoes is enough to make me want to scour the potatoes for bad ones before storing.

Jim ❖ The problem with frosted potatoes is that the tuber cells break down, leaking their contents of sugars and starches. These nutrients are ideal for the growth of soft-rot bacteria (*Erwinia carot*) that quickly multiply and invade healthy tubers. A sure sign of bacterial soft-rot is the soupy mass of watery potatoes combined with a characteristic putrid odour of the bacteria and decaying tubers.

Winter and summer squash

Summer Squash
crookneck
scallop
vegetable marrow
vegetable spaghetti
zucchini (small)

Winter Squash
acorn
buttercup
butternut
hubbard
pepper
pumpkin
spaghetti
sweet potato
zucchini (large)

Squash

How do I store squash?

Lois ❖ Winter squash is best stored at about 10°C and 50–70 percent relative humidity. Storage life varies from variety to variety. Most summer squash does not store well.

A guideline for determining whether a squash will store well is to try to pierce the outer skin with your thumbnail. If you nail easily penetrates the skin, the squash will not keep (and, in the case of winter squash, is immature and will not taste very good). If the skin is firm and your nail does not easily pierce it, the squash is mature and ready for storage.

CHAPTER 6 ❧
TROUBLESHOOTING

One year, we were puzzled by the
failure of our squash plants to
germinate. We sowed twice
with no success, then returned to the
field for one final try. This time,
Ted heard something behind him as
he walked along the row, sowing.
He turned to look and saw a murder
of crows hot on his heels, pecking at
the ground, eating every seed
he'd planted. The solution was simple:
we waited until there were no crows in
sight before our final, successful planting!

Insects

How can I minimize insect problems in my garden?

Lois ❖ You'll never be able to avoid bugs entirely, but you're much better off whenever you can catch a problem early. I take a good look at my plants (this includes looking under the leaves) every time I visit my garden. If I see a few bugs, I pick them off the plant and squish them. If I spot some aphids, I grab my spray bottle of insecticidal soap.

Jim ❖ Insects and diseases often strike plants that are stressed. If you keep your garden clean and give your plants proper care, you'll avoid many problems. That's not to say that you'll avoid pests entirely, but the problems will be substantially reduced.

If you constantly have a disease problem in one part of your garden, you might consider planting more resistant varieties. For example, tomatoes are often listed with "VFN" after the variety name, indicating that the variety is resistant to three serious pests: verticillium, fusarium, and nematodes.

Do any companion plants deter insects?

Jim ❖ Marigolds provide some protection against nematodes. These small worm-like pests attack a wide variety of vegetables. Other links between pest-deterring plants and vegetables are more tenuous.

Instead of looking for companion plants, simply focus on planting a wide variety of vegetables. You will attract a wide variety of beneficial insects, which will help you combat vegetable pests.

Why do my vegetables topple over in June? They seem to be chopped down at ground level.

Jim ❖ That sounds like cutworms, the larval stage of several moth species. In August, the moths lay eggs directly on garden soils. The following May and June, the eggs hatch and the cutworms begin wreaking havoc in gardens. Cutworms are rather indiscriminate when it comes to feeding. They will literally sever every growing plant, vegetable, or weed they encounter. I've witnessed entire fields of young plants decimated in a few days by these voracious worms.

mould on red onions

If I apply dehydrated lime to my vegetable garden, will it help get rid of cutworm eggs?

Jim ❖ Unfortunately, lime has little effect on cutworms. Don't apply lime unless a soil test indicates that it's needed. Too much lime can be as detrimental as too little.

How do I keep the green worms off my broccoli, cauliflower, and cabbage?

Lois ❖ Cabbage worms, the larvae of the cabbage butterfly, are a serious pest of cabbage, cauliflower and broccoli. The best way to avoid worms is to prevent the butterflies from laying eggs on your vegetables. Early in the season, cover the plants with a thin, finely woven white polyester fabric such as Remay cloth. This allows light and moisture to reach the plants but keeps the butterflies at a safe distance.

Several insecticides, both chemical (permethrin) and organic (rotenone) work well if you apply them early. *Bacillus thuringiensis*, a biological control, is also excellent. However, if you can keep the butterflies off your plants, you will keep the worms out of your vegetables.

Which bug killers can I spray on my vegetables the day before I eat them?

Jim ❖ Read the label on your pesticide container. Never eat vegetables treated with any kind of pesticide until the label tells you that it is safe.

When applying any pesticide to your vegetables, whether chemical or organic, there are a few points to remember:

- Read the label to see if the pesticide is registered for use on vegetables.
- Check the "days to harvest" label. The number of days (or possibly hours) indicates the interval between application and safe consumption. If it's five days, for example, you must not consume the vegetables until at least five days have passed after applying the pesticide.
- Don't over-apply or under-apply the product. More is not better! The rate listed on the label has been thoroughly tested and will control the pests.
- Follow all safety precautions listed on the label.

My onions, cabbage, broccoli, and Brussels sprouts always get root maggots. Why?

Lois ❖ The cabbage maggot has been a nuisance in my garden for as long as I can remember. There's nothing more disheartening than watching cabbages topple over and die when maggots attack their roots.

Jim ❖ Cabbage maggots overwinter as pupae in suitable hiding spots around the garden. The adult flies emerge in early spring and seek out cruciferous plants like cabbage, cauliflower, broccoli, and Brussels sprouts. The flies begin to lay eggs around these plants at about the same time as saskatoon bushes bloom. Once the eggs hatch, the maggots tunnel into the root system.

If you have had problems in the past with cabbage maggots, apply insecticide to the soil around your cabbages about the time that cherries, plums, and saskatoons bloom. Granular soil insecticide, applied at the time of planting, can also help, although most plants will still suffer some attack. Interestingly, transplants are attacked to a greater extent than plants that have been sown from seed.

How do I get rid of slugs in the garden?

Lois ❖ The best methods are preventive. First, keep your yard clean. Don't give the slugs a place to hide! If you have only a few slugs, you may be able to get rid of them simply by hand-picking. You can also try slug bait or shop for slug-resistant plants.

Jim ❖ Slugs love to lurk in moist, shady spots: under decks, rock piles, railway ties, and similar out-of-the-way hideouts. If you have a lot of slugs, Safer's Slug and Snail Bait controls them organically. You can also use any slug bait that has metaldehyde as an active ingredient. Metaldehyde can be poisonous to animals, though, so put it in a container that is inaccessible to pets.

How do I control aphids? They're on my leaf lettuce!

Lois ❖ Aphids are a problem in everyone's garden at one time or another. Although they don't cause huge amounts of damage to plants, aphids have a rather unfortunate habit of winding up in your salad!

To control aphids, check your plants often, beginning early in the season. Aphids, it seems, explode in population overnight. Mild insecticides like insecticidal soap are effective if sprayed at the beginning of an outbreak. If you still end up with aphids, simply wash your lettuce thoroughly in the sink before putting it into the salad bowl.

Jim ❖ When you spot aphids, spray affected plants with insecticidal soap, making sure not to miss the undersides of the leaves. Insecticidal soap causes little harm to aphid predators like lacewings and ladybugs. You can also try to attract more ladybugs to your garden, since they prey on aphids. Ladybug lures are available at most garden centres.

My yard seems to have become instantly infested with aphids. Where did they all come from?

Jim ❖ Aphids really do seem to come out of nowhere! Some aphid species lay eggs on tree trunks in the fall. These hatch once the weather warms in the spring. Other aphid species can literally "blow in," riding the winds from the Gulf of Mexico. Aphids reproduce very rapidly, especially during warm, dry weather. They are parthenogenetic, meaning that the females don't require males in order to produce offspring. During the summer, aphids give birth to live young, not eggs, making reproduction that much quicker. An aphid can actually be "pregnant" when it is born!

There are many different species of aphids: green peach aphid, foxglove aphid, melon aphid, and honeysuckle aphid, to name just a few. However, they all respond comparably to the same treatment. Try diatomaceous earth or insecticidal soap if the infestation is light. If you need stronger controls, several other pesticides are effective, but always read the label and apply as recommended. Again, your best defence is a good offence: keep your garden as healthy as possible.

The retired fellow living next door uses rhubarb spray to fight aphids. Does this work?

Jim ❖ I've never tried it, but quite a few organic gardeners claim that homemade rhubarb spray kills aphids and other harmful insects. To make it, they steep rhubarb leaves in boiling water and strain the liquid. Rhubarb leaves contain a very bitter-tasting toxic chemical called calcium oxalate. This may be the active ingredient in your neighbour's spray. No information exists on the safety of rhubarb extract on vegetables, so use it at your discretion.

Rhubarb spray is only one example of many homemade concoctions used by organic gardeners. Remember, though, that just because a product is "organic" doesn't mean it's safe. Judge each pest-control product based on its own merit.

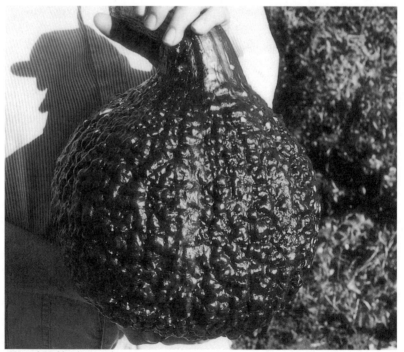

'Warted Hubbard' squash

Animals

How do I keep animals out of my garden?

Jim ❖ Stout, sturdy fencing keeps out dogs and some wildlife. Cacti and sharp rocks discourage many animal pests. You can buy animal repellents at many garden centres and pet stores. You might also consider buying a motion-activated sprinkler.

How do I keep squirrels and birds away from my peas?

Lois ❖ Many garden centres sell specialized netting to put over the vegetables. It is inexpensive and reusable, and birds won't become trapped in the netting. Squirrels are more ingenious at bypassing screening material, but give it a try.

Rabbits are eating my lettuce. How can I get rid of them?

Jim ❖ There are three ways to control rabbits: exclusion, repulsion, and removal. Exclusion is the best method. Use a 60-cm wide chicken wire secured tightly to the ground. That will stop most rabbits. Make sure the mesh size is 2.5 cm or less. Repellants containing Thiram will also fend off rabbits quite effectively. Live traps are effective for small populations, but the issue of what to do with the trapped rabbit can be a problem!

Other Troubles

I added composted farm yard manure and now my vegetables won't grow. What's wrong?

Lois ❖ The manure was likely too fresh. Fresh manure contains high levels of salts. These can severely reduce seed germination or burn the roots of established plants. To prevent burning, use only well-rotted manure and apply it at the recommended rate. But don't worry, the problem is not permanent. The manure should be fully composted by next growing season.

Why didn't my seeds come up? I was growing them in a 2 x 2 x 4 cold frame.

Lois ❖ Despite their name, cold frames often aren't very cold at all! When we first started growing tomatoes, we often found that the cold frames produced soft, spindly, gangly seedlings. There was simply *too much* heat for the plants to form sturdy, stocky stems and foliage. We needed light and some heat, but we also need to circulate the air inside the cold frames to make the plants grow properly.

Jim ❖ Think of the way your car heats up in the sun, even on a relatively cool spring day. On a sunny day, temperatures inside a cold frame can quickly soar to 50°C or higher, effectively cooking your seedlings.

If you use a cold frame, it must be equipped with a roof that can be opened or a fan that can push hot air out and pull cool air in.

What happens to a plant when it freezes?

Jim ❖ It depends on the vegetable. In frost-sensitive vegetables like cucumbers, the water within the plant cells freezes and expands, bursting the cell walls. Later, when the plant thaws, the cell contents leak out, and the plant rapidly dehydrates. Frost-tolerant plants have different ways of coping with freezing temperatures. Some move the water into spaces between the cells, where it can do little harm when it freezes. Others increase the content of sugars or salts within the cells, thus lowering the freezing point and avoiding damage.

My plants are turning yellow and going limp. What could be causing this?

Lois ❖ It sounds as if your soil is waterlogged. Be careful not to overwater your garden. If you're not watering too frequently, you may need to improve your soil's drainage by adding organic matter.

Jim ❖ You can determine if drainage is the problem by grabbing and squeezing a handful of your moist soil. If it compacts into a muddy, clay-like ball, your soil probably has inadequate drainage. If you're growing your vegetables in containers, ensure that the pots all have drainage holes.

Properly drained soil allows excess water to pass through, leaving tiny air spaces. If this doesn't happen, the soil becomes waterlogged, displacing oxygen that is needed by the roots. Above ground, this translates into yellow, wilted foliage.

Why do my spinach and radishes bolt?

Jim ❖ Both spinach and radish are long-day plants. When the day length reaches a certain duration (14 hours) these plants are triggered to produce a long flower stalk. If the day length stays shorter than 14 hours, spinach and radish don't bolt (go to seed). Heat can also increase bolting.

Look for bolt-resistant varieties of spinach. Although not perfect, they are considerably better than the older varieties. Another strategy is to plant early so that your spinach and radishes can be harvested before the long, hot days of summer arrive. I like to plant spinach late in the season: the shorter days and cooler nights of late summer and early fall are ideal for growth.

My peas have powdery mildew. Can I still keep the pods and dry the seeds for next year?

Jim ❖ No. When you collect seed from infected plants, you increase the risk of spreading the disease. Powdery mildew, a fungal disease, can be carried in the seeds. If your peas are hit by powdery mildew, you simply have to absorb your losses and begin again next year with clean, disease-free seed.

Another important point when you have a mildew problem is to ensure that you remove and destroy all the diseased foliage from your garden. Do not work it back in to the soil or put it in your compost pile, or the fungus may cause problems for you again next year.

My garden was ravaged by hail. Will the plants recover?

Lois ❖ Some plants are more resilient than others. All you can do is wait to see which plants will come back and which will perish. Potatoes recover very well from hail damage, particularly early in the season. Young bean plants, on the other hand, can easily be destroyed.

Give hail-ravaged plants several days before you decide to start over. They look worst right after the hailstorm, but will often bounce back surprisingly well.

It snowed last night and I was unable to cover my vegetables. Will they be okay?

Lois ❖ You might assume that an unexpected snowstorm would be the worst thing that could happen to your vegetables. In fact, it's often the proverbial blessing in disguise.

Jim ❖ Seed germination and seedling emergence are usually improved by a spring snowfall! If it snows just after you sow your vegetable seeds, moisture will slowly infiltrate the soil as the snow melts. Snow also acts as an insulator, protecting plants from frost if the skies clear at night. The best snow for young plants is light and fluffy. Heavy, wet snow might sometimes break the branches of larger plants. And, of course, snow will injure frost-sensitive vegetables like cucumbers, pumpkins, okra, and sweet potatoes. Frost and prolonged cold after the snowfall are far worse than the snow itself.

Will Killex hurt my vegetable garden?

Jim ❖ Yes! Lawn weed-killers contain selective herbicides designed to kill broadleaf plants while sparing lawn grasses. Don't apply them anywhere near your vegetable garden or flowerbeds on windy days. 2,4-D drifts and can cause tremendous damage even when it is not sprayed directly on your plants. If you apply lawn weed-killers directly to vegetables (corn is an exception because it is a grass), you will severely injure them, or even kill them.

It's not even safe to apply the herbicide before sowing seeds or transplanting vegetables. Herbicides like 2,4-D and Mecoprop typically persist in the soil for three or four months—in other words, one growing season. During that time, the chemicals can still be absorbed by the vegetable roots.

Mushrooms have sprung up on my lawn. Can I eat them?

Lois ❖ Do not eat any mushroom from your yard unless it can be positively identified as edible. If you're interested in growing your own fresh mushrooms, most garden centres carry kits that will get you started safely.

'Kilima' leek

CHAPTER 7 ❦
VEGETABLE VARIETIES

Each vegetable has its own quirks.
A treatment that works for one vegetable
may not be the right answer for another.
Some plants require comparatively little
effort to grow; others will need close
attention throughout the season.
Puzzled by a new situation? Longing
to try a new variety or vegetable,
but uncertain how to proceed? This
section may help to answer some
particularly vexing questions or give you
insights into plants you haven't tried yet!

Artichokes

Can we grow globe artichokes in western Canada?

Lois ❖ Globe artichokes grow very well in most regions and do not require a long season to mature. Always start artichokes from transplants. Artichokes transplant easily, grow rapidly, and suffer few pest problems.

Jim ❖ Artichokes enjoy temperatures of 15–24°C and begin to suffer when the heat reaches above 30°C. They can also survive heavy frosts, making them an excellent choice for Canadian gardeners.

What are those little black bugs on the leaves of my artichokes?

Jim ❖ Blackbean aphids are among the few pests that attack artichokes. These tiny black insects accumulate on the newest growing points of the plants. A good spray with insecticidal soap will control them, provided you catch the problem early.

These aphids can cause the artichoke heads to curl when the insects move from the leaves to the heads. Aphids also leave behind a sticky residue called "honeydew."

What's a good fertilizer for artichokes?

Jim ❖ Although artichokes will perform well in lower-fertility soils, they need plenty of nitrogen to produce high yields. A 30-10-10 fertilizer is an excellent choice.

Asparagus

If I plant asparagus roots, can I harvest some in the first year?

Lois ❖ No matter how tempted you are, don't pick a single spear until your asparagus has become well established. The rule is to harvest no spears the first year of transplanting, just a little the second year, then enjoy a full harvest the third and subsequent years. You'll be well rewarded for your patience!

Should I cut off the fern-like growths from my asparagus plants?

Jim ❖ The fern-like growths are actually modified stems that produce food for the following year's shoots, so leave them on until fall. You can remove the dead ferns in the fall for an easier harvest the following year.

Asparagus crowns produce shoots in what's called a "dominant hierarchy" system. When you harvest one spear, you signal the crown to send up another one. In general, the earliest buds produce the largest spears, and the size drops off gradually after that. Once you notice that the new spears are noticeably thinner than the early spears, stop harvesting and allow the remaining spears to grow into ferns. Unless you leave some growth to feed the roots, the crown will weaken and may eventually die.

I really like asparagus, but I've never grown it before. What do I do?

Lois ❖ First, choose big, healthy crowns. The larger the crown, the more vigorous the resulting plant. Plant the crowns 15–20 cm deep in a furrow. Deeper planting produces fewer, larger shoots; shallow planting produces thinner, more numerous shoots. Fill the furrow as the plants grow.

When you harvest in the second year (never in the first year!), harvest for only 3 weeks and choose spears no smaller than 0.5 cm in diameter. Asparagus plants come in male and female. The female plants produce larger spears but lower yields because of the energy needed for seed production.

Jim ❖ The "crown" of asparagus refers to the part of the plant where the roots join the stem. When you purchase asparagus roots from your garden centre, you will notice that each "plant" is actually a cluster of long roots joined at the topmost part—the crown.

Remember that asparagus is a perennial vegetable, so it is crucial to prepare the planting area properly. Dig out an area 60 cm wide and 60 cm deep to the desired length of your row. Mix in plenty of peat moss or compost to ensure that the tilth of the soil is loose and rich. And always choose a weed-free location, even if this means delaying your planting for a season or two.

Beans

Some of my beans emerged but never developed true leaves. Why?

Jim ❖ When a bean seed is cracked, the embryo within is often injured. If the growing point has been damaged, a seedling might still emerge, but it will immediately stop growing. This is called a blind plant. It will never grow into a mature plant and should be removed.

My beans become all rusty in the summer. Why?

Jim ❖ The rusty-looking beans have likely succumbed to a disease called common bacterial blight. People walking through the bean patch while the beans are covered with dew or during wet weather can easily spread bacterial diseases. We've had problems with this disease in our garden simply from being too impatient and harvesting in wet conditions. There is a disease called rust that attacks beans, but it is uncommon.

The ends of my beans rot. Why?

Jim ❖ When bean pods touch the ground, they can become infected with a disease called white mould. The moist soil provides the ideal environment for infection by this disease. Cotton-like fungus grows over the bean, usually starting at soil level. The infection can kill the plant in humid climates, although it is less virulent in drier areas.

Space the rows to allow plenty of air movement, and add mulch to keep the beans from contacting the soil. You might also want to try a bean variety with an open canopy and a more upright growth habit that keeps the pods off the ground.

Beets

My beets have white rings inside. Why?

Lois ❖ White rings are usually caused by too much or too little water, extreme temperatures, or any other factors that stress the plant. White rings can also appear if the beets go to seed, usually during a very hot spell. This is also referred to as "woodiness" because of the tougher texture and bitter taste. Some varieties are more prone to white rings than others.

Jim ❖ The problem can be particularly bad when the beets suffer stress at the fifth leaf stage of growth—usually midsummer. Be sure to water transplants well, especially during hot spells, to minimize this problem. Some varieties inherently have white rings; this is not a disorder in these vareties.

My beets get too big. What do I do?

Lois ❖ If you plant your beets thinly, they develop bigger roots simply because they have more room and less competition. If you want smaller beets, simply sow them more thickly. You can also begin to harvest your beets earlier. Beets are very tasty even when they're small.

Another trick I use is to sow only a small patch of beets early in the season, and then seed more beets every three weeks until mid July. The later-sown beets are smaller and don't grow as quickly toward the end of the season.

Why do my beet roots have black spots in the centre?

Lois ❖ I remember this problem showing up in our fields after years of sowing beets without seeing it. It took us a while to determine that our soil had become depleted of a micronutrient called boron.

Jim ❖ This condition, called heart rot or black heart, is caused by a deficiency of boron. Soils that are very acidic or very alkaline often have boron problems, as do dry soils. Test your soil's pH and correct it if necessary. And be sure to water your beets regularly.

You can also use fertilizers that contain trace elements including boron. Borax will also correct the problem, but be careful. It's very easy to overdose with Borax, and too much can severely injure crops. More is not better!

Can my beets tolerate frost or should I harvest them now?

Lois ❖ Beet roots are very frost tolerant. However, if you want to eat the beet tops, you should harvest them before fall frost. Frost doesn't kill beet tops but it makes them tough and bitter.

Jim ❖ Long spells of cool weather (temperatures of 10°C for 2–3 weeks) may cause beets to bolt (go to seed).

Why are my beets scabby?

Jim ❖ Like potatoes, beets can get scab-producing disease (*Streptomyces scabies*). This soil-borne disease attacks the roots just below soil level. It's usually only a minor problem, but it can affect the surface appearance of the roots.

Broccoli

My broccoli has started to produce yellow flowers. Why? How can I prevent it?

Lois ❖ Unless you harvest it in a timely manner, every broccoli plant will eventually flower. However, this can happen prematurely if the plants are exposed to extended periods of hot, dry weather. Many of the newer hybrid varieties are more resistant to flowering, but some poorer varieties flower very quickly.

Jim ❖ Commercial growers harvest at the tight-bud stage, when the head feels very firm. Broccoli that is harvested at loose-bud stage can flower even if it is stored in a fridge or cooler.

Why does my broccoli have hollow stems?

Lois ❖ Hollow stem is a common problem in broccoli and cauliflower. It happens when the plant grows too quickly. The flavour is not affected, however, and it's still perfectly edible.

Jim ❖ Hollow stems usually develop because of excessive nitrogen in the soil or because the plants are too widely spaced. Keep moisture levels consistent and ease off on high-nitrogen fertilizers. An imbalance between boron and nitrogen can also cause hollow stems.

Brussels sprouts

Will frost hurt my Brussels sprouts?

Lois ❖ On the contrary! Mature Brussels sprouts improve in flavour after several hard frosts, so don't be in a rush to harvest them. They're very frost tolerant.

Jim ❖ The only time to worry about moderately hard frosts on Brussels sprouts is in the spring. If the plant has grown "soft" indoors and is transplanted without hardening off, it may be injured by frost.

Why do my Brussels sprouts die after I transplant them?

Lois ❖ This is one of the most disheartening diseases of Brussels sprouts. The seedlings look good but just don't seem to grow. When you check the stem, it looks as if it has been pinched off, and you know its days are numbered.

Jim ❖ Transplanted Brussels sprouts often suffer from a disease called wire stem (*Rhizoctonia solani*). The stem darkens and the outer layer dies, leaving a thin, wire-like portion that often breaks in the wind. Once plants develop wire stem, they remain stunted and eventually die. Chemical controls are useless once the disease is evident. There are currently no varieties resistant against this disease. Use high-quality seed in rich, well-drained soil and keep the garden soil as disease-free as possible by disposing of diseased plants and rotating crops.

Cabbage

How do I stop my cabbage from splitting?

Lois ❖ Early, tender varieties often split as they mature, particularly after periods of heavy rain. Late-season cabbage rarely, if ever, splits.

Jim ❖ Be sure to water regularly and avoid sporadic heavy watering. A period of drought when the heads are forming rapidly, followed by heavy irrigation, makes splitting worse on early-season cabbage.

Why do the interior leaves of my cabbage have brown edges?

Lois ❖ This is usually a problem related to water, not disease. You can simply trim off the affected leaves if the problem is minor. However, if the problem is severe, it's nearly impossible to remove all the brown edges because of the way the leaves are folded.

Jim ❖ The internal leaves of cabbage can turn brown at the tops for two reasons: a lack of water and a shortage of calcium. Usually it's a combination of the two. Plant cells die and turn brown without calcium, and without enough water the calcium can't find its way to the leaf edges. Add lime to the soil to solve the calcium problem, and water your cabbage regularly when the heads are filling out.

What causes the brown, corky patches on my cabbage leaves?

Jim ❖ When thrips feed on cabbage leaves, they leave behind corky brown patches. These tiny, slender insects wedge their way into the small spaces between leaves to feed. Thrips are thigmotactic insects, meaning they like the security of having leaves pressing up against their bodies.

Once the corky brown spots are there, there's nothing you can do. If you've had thrips in the past, use a preventive spray such as malathion early in the season to get rid of them before they become established.

My husband just cut off the big leaves of my cabbages. Will they still grow?

Lois ❖ Tell that man to leave your cabbages alone! He hasn't killed them, but he has lowered your yield.

Jim ❖ Leaves are food factories powered by sunlight. The more leaves you remove, the less the plant will produce. Large leaves that are vibrant and green produce tremendous amounts of sugars for the developing cabbage heads. Removing them reduces the yield, and the open wounds are an invitation to insects and disease.

Are cabbages damaged by frost?

Lois ❖ Cabbage is very frost tolerant. Over the years, I've often had to scrape snow off cabbage heads to harvest them. If temperatures are extremely cold at harvest, say −5°C, immediately place the cabbages in the fridge and allow them to thaw gradually. The heads may be damaged if they warm up too quickly.

Jim ❖ As with Brussels sprouts and other cruciferous vegetables, the only time to worry about light frosts is in the spring, and only if the seedlings haven't been properly hardened off.

Why are my cabbage heads brown on the bottom?

Lois ❖ Cabbage root maggots have always been the worst insect problem on my cabbage, particularly on transplanted cabbage. They can ruin a crop in very short order.

Jim ❖ Cabbage heads turn brown on the bottom for a couple of reasons. Cabbage root maggots (*Delia radicum*) destroy roots and often tunnel into the stem core later in the season. The maggots can also tunnel their way up to the base of the lower leaves. A fungal disease called crown rot (*Rhizoctonia* spp.) can also cause bottom rot. This disease resides in the soil and attacks any leaves that touch the ground.

Can I eat ornamental cabbage?

Lois ❖ Yes, you can eat ornamental cabbage, but it is nowhere near as tender or tasty as the garden varieties. Ornamental cabbage also produces significantly lower yields than the typical garden varieties.

Jim ❖ Ornamental cabbage is really just a coloured kale. The term "ornamental cabbage" simply describes the leaf shape.

Carrots

What causes carrots to fork?

Lois ❖ When a growing root comes up against particularly hard ground, it responds by splitting into two or more branches. To prevent this problem, always work the soil deeply and add lots of organic matter to clay soils to loosen the earth and improve the tilth of your soil.

Jim ❖ A lack of water can also cause the same problem. If the tiny growing point dies, the carrot will fork. We also noticed carrots forking in soil that had been recently enriched with fresh manure—use only well-rotted (composted) manure on your garden!

What are the black spots on my carrot roots?

Jim ❖ Your carrots probably have a disease called cavity spot (*Pythium* spp.). This fungal disease causes sunken black spots that penetrate a few millimetres below the surface. Excessive fertilizer and waterlogged soil can increase cavity spot.

What are the differences among Nantes, Baby Sweet, and other carrot varieties?

Lois ❖ Carrots fall into these categories:

- Chantenay: medium-sized, stocky, conical roots with large cores
- Danvers: late-season processing carrots, very uniform with good interior colour; roots are broad and tapered, with large, strong tops
- Imperators: long, cylindrical, with tapered roots; traditionally somewhat woody (although with new breeding, many Imperator types have been crossed with Nantes to improve their flavour)
- Nantes: the sweetest and juiciest of all, but shorter and brittle, with blunt ends; great taste and appearance.

Jim ❖ Commercial growers choose carrots based on their ultimate use. Chantenays are high-yielding carrots, but they're very large and not too juicy, so they resist breaking when they're harvested mechanically. They're often the cheapest carrots on the market and easier to process for institutional food use.

Why did many of my carrots crack?

Lois ❖ I've found that the juiciest carrots are the most prone to cracking. Nantes are the best-tasting carrots but also the worst for cracking—that's the price you pay for flavour!

Jim ❖ Growth cracks are the result of fluctuating moisture levels, such as when a heavy rainfall follows an extended dry period. The roots expand so rapidly that they crack. To prevent this, keep soil moisture as even as possible throughout the growing season.

Why do the tops of my carrots look stunted?

Jim ❖ This could be due to a lack of water. However, if you have been watering regularly and the soil is reasonably loose and fertile, the cause could be a disease called Aster Yellows.

Aster Yellows is most common in carrots, but it can also attack celery, eggplant, and lettuce. The disease is spread by insects known as leafhoppers. The leafhoppers don't cause much damage as they feed on the leaves, but they transmit the Aster Yellows, which stunts carrot leaves. The carrot roots are pale and hairy, and their flavour is bitter.

If you control the leafhoppers early in the season, you can stop Aster Yellows. Leafhoppers can be controlled with permethrin- or carbaryl-based insecticides early in the season; Aster Yellows is typically most severe late in the growing season.

My carrots didn't germinate at all. Why?

Lois ❖ Whenever I plant carrots, I always take great care not to "pound" the soil down with heavy applications of water. Once the soil is crusted, it's almost impossible for the seedling to push through the surface.

Jim ❖ When seedlings don't emerge from the ground in reasonable numbers, it's tempting to blame the seed. But usually the problem is the seed's environment.

For example, carrot seedlings have a very difficult time pushing through soils with hard crusts; many die before they emerge. And soils that are too dry at the critical period of germination will cause seedlings to dry up and die. To avoid these problems, keep seedbeds consistently moist—neither saturated nor dry.

What is carrot rust fly? Why do I have it? How do I get rid of it?

Jim ❖ Carrot rust fly is very common in some regions and rare or non-existent in others. British Columbia, Quebec, Ontario, and Newfoundland have major infestations, while it remains a minor problem on the prairies.

Carrot rust flies are attracted to the carbon dioxide emitted by the roots and lay their eggs on the plants. The newly hatched larva tunnel into the roots, damaging the carrots.

Will my carrots freeze in the garden?

Lois ❖ The biggest problem with leaving carrots in the ground is a minor one: the tops die down and the carrots are impossible to pull. You'll need a good garden fork to get the job done. But carrots keep wonderfully in the soil for several weeks after the first frost.

Jim ❖ In the garden, carrot roots are sheltered from the frost by the soil. They can tolerate several degrees of frost without damage. However, the crown region can be injured under severely cold conditions. You can recognize crown injury from the tiny cracks and corky texture of the crown. These frost-damaged carrots will not keep well.

Cauliflower

My cauliflower just produces a small curd. Why?

Lois ❖ Whenever I grew cauliflower transplants and couldn't transplant them into the garden because of poor weather, many of them would button. It was simply due to them becoming rootbound in the seedling flat.

Jim ❖ When cauliflower seedlings become overgrown in the pot, they often initiate curds. Once this happens, the plants always remain stunted. Either seed your cauliflower directly, or be careful not to buy overgrown transplants.

My cauliflower turns yellow as it's growing. Is there any way to prevent this?

Lois ❖ Cauliflower curds turn yellow when exposed to sunlight. If the leaves aren't wrapped around the curd, tie them up with a rubber band. This will help. The good news is that the yellow cauliflower is still perfectly edible. It just doesn't look quite as attractive.

Jim ❖ Look for "self-wrapping" cauliflower varieties. These varieties have lots of leaves that literally wrap around the curd, protecting it from sunlight. The seed of self-wrapping cauliflower is often a little more expensive, but it's well worth the extra few cents.

Celery

How do I get the base of celery to stay white?

Lois ❖ The base of the plant will remain white if it's not exposed to sunlight. Mound up the base or crown region with soil.

Can I eat celery roots?

Lois ❖ Yes! They are quite tasty, either raw or cooked. The flavour is a cross between intense celery and parsley.

My celery was very bitter. What did I do wrong?

Lois ❖ Celery is a finicky vegetable to grow. Underwatering, under-fertilizing, cold, or excessive heat can all contribute to bitter stalks.

Jim ❖ Celery is a heavy feeder—it likes lots of fertilizer and plenty of water. If you don't monitor fertility and moisture levels, you'll often end up with bitter celery.

Chinese cabbage

What's attacking the roots of my Chinese cabbage?

Jim ❖ Root maggots attack many cruciferous species (cabbage, cauliflower, broccoli, etc.), including Chinese cabbage. Small white maggots will be evident in the roots of the cabbage.

A disease called club root (*Plasmodiophora brassicae*) could also be the problem. The disease causes club-like galls to form on the roots. Severely affected roots can't absorb water or nutrients, and the plants remain stunted.

How should I fertilize my Chinese cabbage?

Jim ❖ Chinese cabbage is a moderately heavy feeder. Use a balanced fertilizer like 20-20-20.

Corn

On corn, what do "SS" and "SE" mean?

Lois ❖ These symbols refer to the quantity of sugar in the cob. SS means supersweet. These types have extra sugar, and the sugar breaks down much more slowly after harvest than other varieties. SE means sugar-enhanced.

Sugar-enhanced corn has less sugar than supersweet, but still remains sweet longer than standard corn varieties. The kernels are also much tenderer than SS varieties.

I much prefer SE varieties for fresh eating. The kernels are very tender and sweet. SS varieties are excellent for freezing because they stay firm when thawed.

Why aren't my corncobs thoroughly filled out?

Jim ❖ Spotty filling of corncobs is due to poor pollination. This usually happens when corn is planted in a solitary row rather than in blocks. Corn pollen must land on each thread of silk for complete pollination. Each strand of silk is attached to a single kernel.

Corn breeders constantly strive to develop varieties with good tipfill, an industry buzzword for large, rounded, full cobs. Some of the older varieties don't have great tipfill, while many of the new hybrids have excellent tipfill.

When is corn ready to harvest? Can it tolerate any frost?

Lois ❖ Corn is ready to harvest when the silks are brown and have dried up and you can feel the cobs through the husks. The tip of the cob should be blunt and feel full. The appearance and feel of the finished cobs differ with the variety. It takes a bit of experience to know exactly when the cobs are at their prime, but with time you'll learn.

Jim ❖ Corn will be badly damaged by even a light frost. If frost strikes once the cobs have matured, you have about one week to harvest them before the flavour starts to deteriorate significantly. If frost strikes before the cobs have matured, the corn will not ripen.

Cucumbers

What's the difference between a field cucumber and an ornamental cucumber?

Lois ❖ Although both plants have lots of vines and produce similarly shaped leaves, they are two different species. Garden cucumbers produce edible fruit, while ornamental cucumbers produce a spiky, dry, inedible seedpod.

Jim ❖ Ornamental cucumbers are considered weeds in some areas, but they do produce rather attractive annual vines with interesting spiky, papery seed pods. Although the plants resemble each other when they are small, they are actually completely different species. Wild cucumber vine is *Echinocystis lobata*, while field cucumber is *Cucumis sativis*.

Do cucumbers climb?

Lois ❖ Yes and no. Cucumbers don't have tendrils, the long, thin structures that wrap around poles or framing to support the weight of a plant as it climbs. But cucumbers do have vines that can be woven through lattices or around branches for support. Some gardeners train their cucumbers on trellises to keep the fruit off the ground and conserve space. Greenhouse or long English cucumbers require both support and pruning.

What are gynecious cucumbers?

Jim ❖ Gynecious cucumber plants produce mostly female flowers. Since only female flowers produce fruit, gynecious cucumbers are much higher yielding. In a package of gynecious seeds, a few male pollinators are thrown in to pollinate the female flowers. Typically 85–90 percent are gynecious seed, with 10–15 percent monoecious for pollination.

Why are my cucumber seeds coloured green and red?

Jim ❖ This allows the packagers to determine which seeds are by and large male, and which are by and large female. Male seeds are usually dyed green or blue, while the females are red or pink.

Lois ❖ Many parents still follow a similar principle when dressing their babies!

Why are my cucumbers tapered and bulbous?

Lois ❖ This is often due to lack of water. Cucumbers should get about 3 cm of water each week under normal conditions (more if you're growing in containers).

Jim ❖ Misshapen fruit is often caused by a lack of nutrients, particularly nitrogen and potassium. Don't forget to fertilize! Poor pollination can also produce the same symptoms.

Do I need bees to pollinate cucumbers?

Jim ❖ Bees are essential for proper pollination of garden cucumbers, but long English cucumbers don't need them. For field cucumbers to pollinated successfully, pollen must be physically transferred from one flower to the next. Commercial growers usually place beehives around their fields to ensure good pollination.

However, 'Cool Breeze,' a new variety of field cucumber, sets fruit without pollination. It's a good alternative in locations with few bees around, like a high-rise balcony, and in shorter-season areas with cooler summers, where bees are less prolific and active.

It has been estimated that one bee is required for each plant. Bumblebees are the best pollinators, but honeybees pollinate cucumbers as well.

What cucumber varieties should I grow in my greenhouse?

Lois ❖ Specially bred long English cucumber varieties are best for indoor cultivation.

Regular garden-variety cucumbers grow well in greenhouses, but since they require pollination by insects, bees in particular, they set fruit very poorly indoors. One recently introduced variety, Cool Breeze, doesn't require pollination to produce fruit, so it's a good choice if you want to grow a field cucumber in a greenhouse.

Jim ❖ Long English cucumbers produce very high yields of fruit without pollination. However, they are a challenging crop to grow and require lots of sun, warmth, fertilizer, and water. I've always maintained that if you can grow English cucumbers well, then you can grow any plant well.

Eggplants

My eggplants don't produce very big fruit before frost. Why?

Lois ❖ Eggplant is a long-season crop that enjoys lots of heat. Always grow eggplant in the hottest, sunniest spot in the garden. If your area has a short growing season, I recommend that you plant large transplants to reduce the time to harvest and that you grow them in containers in a sunny, warm, sheltered location.

Jim ❖ Grow the eggplant in a greenhouse *at least* 8 weeks before planting outside. Eggplant grows poorly at temperatures below 16°C; 20–25°C is best.

What's eating my eggplant?

Lois ❖ Eggplants are closely related to potatoes and are vulnerable to many of the same pests. The Colorado potato beetle, for instance, can destroy an eggplant crop in short order.

Jim ❖ Cutworms are also bad for chewing off the plants at soil level.

Is there such a thing as white eggplant?

Lois ❖ Yes, white eggplant is simply a variety of eggplant. 'Casper' and 'White Beauty' are two popular varieties.

Jim ❖ There are also yellow, apple-green, and even pink varieties.

Garlic

What is the difference between elephant garlic and regular garlic?

Lois ❖ Elephant garlic is actually a species of leek, but it produces huge, garlic-like cloves. It also has a much milder flavour than regular garlic, but it does not store as well.

Jim ❖ Onions, garlic, leeks, and shallots are all members of the *Allium* genus in the Liliaceae family:

- *Allium ampeloprasum*: leek
- *Allium sativum*: garlic
- *Allium schoenoprasum*: chive

- *Allium cepa* L. Cepa group: common onion
- *Allium cepa* L. Aggregatum group: shallot
- *Allium cepa* L. Proliferum group: Egyptian onion
- *Allium fistulosum*: Welsh onion.

Why are my garlic tops turning brown or black and shrivelling up?

Jim ❖ Garlic can suffer from several bacterial and fungal diseases. One of the more common fungal diseases is neck rot, caused by *Botrytis* spp. It infects the neck region where the bulb joins the leaves. It's not uncommon to lose half the bulbs in storage if this disease is not controlled. This problem is more common when conditions are abnormally wet. Before storing, cure the garlic by subjecting it to warm, dry air for a couple of weeks (until the skins are dry).

If your garlic tops are shrivelling up, remove any affected bulbs. To avoid the problem in the future, always buy and plant plump, firm, disease-free garlic bulbs.

Kale

I've heard that kale is edible. Is that true?

Lois ❖ Yes, kale is edible, and very nutritious, I might add.

Jim ❖ Kale is one of the most nutritious vegetables. A 100-g serving of kale provides 100 percent of an adult's daily requirement of vitamins A and C, and 13 percent of the calcium. Kale is delicious steamed and served with butter or vinegar. Young, tender leaves are tastiest.

Some small beetles are attacking my kale leaves. What are they?

Jim ❖ Flea beetles chew tiny holes through the young leaves of kale plants, making them look like they've been hit by a shotgun. Early-season flea-beetle control with permethrin or rotenone can solve this problem. Be sure to read the product label carefully before applying the pesticide.

Is ornamental kale the same as edible kale?

Lois ❖ Unlike regular kale, ornamental kale has been bred for its outstanding colours. It is edible but not terribly tasty.

Kohlrabi

Will kohlrabi tolerate frost?

Lois ❖ Kohlrabi is very frost tolerant and can be seeded or transplanted in the early spring.

Jim ❖ I have yet to lose a direct-seeded kohlrabi crop to any degree of spring frost. The seed can be planted as soon as the soil can be worked. Kohlrabi can also be left in the garden for several weeks after the first fall frost.

Why does my kohlrabi split?

Lois ❖ Like many vegetables, kohlrabi will develop growth cracks when a heavy rain follows a dry spell. To prevent the problem, do your best to keep the soil evenly moist.

Fortunately, split kohlrabi heals quickly, and the problem doesn't affect the flavour. All you'll lose is aesthetics, because the split surface takes on a corky appearance—but since you have to peel kohlrabi to eat it, the outer appearance is irrelevant.

What are the small black beetles eating my kohlrabi?

Jim ❖ Flea beetles attack virtually all members of the cruciferous family: mustard greens, rutabaga, kale, cauliflower, cabbage, Brussels sprouts, broccoli, bok choy, turnip, radish. You can spray with rotenone, carbaryl, or permethrin early in the season if you have had this problem in previous years.

Leeks

What's the difference between leeks and onions?

Jim ❖ Leek and onion are both members of the lily family, but they are two distinct species: leeks are *Allium ampeloprasum* and onions are *Allium cepa*. Leeks tend to have a milder, more subtle flavour than onions.

What type of soil do leeks require?

Lois ❖ Leeks are fairly heavy feeders, but they are rather shallowly rooted. They do best in well-fertilized soil, rich in organic matter.

Jim ❖ Leeks, like all members of the genus *Allium*, are poor competitors with weeds. A clean, weed-free soil is essential for good yields.

Can leeks tolerate frost?

Lois ❖ Leeks are very frost tolerant and can withstand temperatures several degrees below freezing.

Lettuce

Why is my lettuce bitter?

Lois ❖ This is usually caused by a lack of water, abnormally hot or cold weather, or insufficient fertilizer. Whenever lettuce suffers a check in its growth (that is, a stress), the potential for bitterness increases. Some varieties tend to be bitterer than others, so you may want to try growing an assortment of varieties to see which you prefer.

Jim ❖ Lettuce likes cool temperatures (15–18°C). At temperatures in the upper 20s, lettuce suffers, particularly if the nights are also warm. Some hot regions are unsuitable for head lettuce production in the peak of summer.

How close should I sow my lettuce seed?

Lois ❖ I like to plant all types of lettuce quite thickly. I begin to thin the seedlings when they are very small and I use them in salads. As the remaining seedlings grow, I "re-thin" them to a greater spacing. This way I have a constant supply of fresh lettuce for a longer period, and I can take full advantage of my garden space.

Jim ❖ It depends on the type of lettuce you are growing. You can sow leaf lettuce much more thickly than head lettuce. With head lettuce, commercial growers typically space plants 20–25 cm apart in the row, with 40–60 cm between rows.

Can I still start leaf lettuce from seed in mid July?

Lois ❖ Absolutely! You can begin harvesting leaf lettuce a few weeks after sowing the seeds, so you still have plenty of time.

I start planting lettuce as soon as I can work the soil in the spring, and then plant more every week until early August. If you plant a little bit of lettuce every two or three weeks, you'll have a steady supply of young, tender leaves throughout the growing season.

Jim ❖ To plan a succession of leaf lettuce harvesting, first determine how much leaf lettuce you and your family need. Let's say you expect to consume a 150-cm row of lettuce each week for 10 weeks. In that case, you would need a 1.5-m row or two 0.75-m rows or three 0.5-m rows, etc. In the first week, sow a 150-cm row of lettuce seed and stop. Keep the unplanted portion of the row tilled and weed free, then plant another 150-cm row every 2 or 3 weeks. Some plantings will grow better than others, but overall, you'll enjoy more of the fresh young lettuce that succession planting offers.

Midsummer planting is a bit risky because of the July and August heat, but it's still worth the gamble. High temperatures may result in poor-quality lettuce, but lettuce seed is inexpensive and the potential loss of a few lettuce plants is outweighed by the harvest of tender new leaves.

Melons

How can I make my melons mature more quickly?

Jim ❖ Melons prefer a long, warm growing season. Anything that you can do to increase heat helps. If you can, locate melons on a south to southwest facing slope. If you don't have a slope, make a mound of soil and plant them on top. This allows the sun's rays to heat the plants at a more direct angle. Cover the plants at night with a lightweight fabric to trap heat. Hot caps early in the season also help.

Can temperature affect the number of female blooms on a melon plant?

Jim ❖ Long days combined with cool temperatures cause melons to produce more pistillate (female) flowers. If you experience a run of several consecutive long, cool days, pinch off a few of the tiny fruit to redirect the plant's energy into producing fewer, larger melons and ensure that some fruit will mature.

Can I train melons on a trellis?

Lois ❖ Yes, you can weave the vines through or tie them to the trellis. Ensure that the plants receive lots of sunlight, and use slings to securely support the weight of the maturing fruit.

How much sunlight do melons need?

Lois ❖ As much as they can get! If you can, choose a location that receives direct sunlight from morning to night.

Jim ❖ Any amount of shade, particularly in cooler regions, can make the difference between getting a crop and waiting until next year. In cooler zones, you must make every effort to capture heat and light. That means providing sun from morning to night, avoiding planting in low areas, and covering the plants on cool nights.

Mesclun

What is mesclun?

Lois ❖ Mesclun is simply a potpourri of young salad leaves. Blends vary, but they may include arugula, radicchio, sorrel, several types of lettuce, and even the edible weed lamb's quarters.

Jim ❖ Mesclun is intended to be cut en masse rather than selecting out individual plants, and scissors are the best tool to use. That way you have an instant tossed salad! Keep the mesclun patch clean prior to planting to avoid harvesting weeds with your greens. I like to plant mesclun in a block rather than in long rows for easier harvest and more efficient use of my garden space.

Onions

Does adding sulphur to the soil help onions?

Lois ❖ It may, but don't add sulphur to soils that are already quite acidic: sulphur further acidifies the soil.

Jim ❖ The onion's characteristic odour and flavour derives from a class of chemicals called isothiocyanates. Sulphur is one element of isothiocyanates. Increasing sulphur in soil has been shown to increase flavour in some cases.

When should I harvest my onions?

Lois ❖ It depends on the type of onion. You can harvest green onions anytime, but I like to wait until the stalks are about 1 cm wide. Some onion varieties make excellent green onions if you harvest them early, then develop into nice cooking or slicing onions if you allow them to grow to maturity.

Jim ❖ You can harvest cooking onions once the bulbs are an acceptable size. However, if you plan on storing them, leave them in the ground until they reach their maximum size and the necks have fallen over and dried.

If you harvest onions for storage before the necks are dry, they will sprout and rot. After you dig the onions up, leave them on the soil surface to dry in the sun before putting them into storage. Cure onions at 24°C or warmer for at least a week. If the weather is poor, spread them out on a deck and keep them sheltered from the rain. Store once they are dry.

Parsnips

I've heard that parsnip leaves will irritate hands. Is this true?

Lois ❖ I've harvested parsnips for years without gloves. No one I know has had this problem.

Jim ❖ Yes. Parsnips contain chemicals called psoralens that, if rubbed on the skin, make the skin photosensitive (in other words, more vulnerable to ultraviolet light). People sensitive to psoralens may also develop large, painful blisters. If you are sensitive, wear gloves when handling parsnip foliage. Like Mom, I've never had a problem with parsnips.

Why do my parsnips turn brown when I wash them?

Jim ❖ Parsnips grown in sandy soils can suffer abrasion injury from the sand particles. After you wash the parsnips, the exposed flesh begins to oxidize and turn brown—much like a cut apple left on the counter.

Lois ❖ The browning has no effect on the quality or flavour of the washed parsnips. They just don't look as nice.

Can I leave parsnips in the ground after a frost?

Lois ❖ Yes. In fact, the taste of parsnips improves after several hard frosts. Parsnips are one of the most frost tolerant of all vegetables. The roots can even overwinter in the soil when air temperatures are down to the -30°C range.

Peas

Do peas need to be pollinated?

Lois ❖ Yes. But peas are almost entirely self-pollinated. They don't require any outside help!

Jim ❖ Peas need to be pollinated, but not cross-pollinated; that is, they can successfully pollinate themselves. Not all plants are able to self-pollinate. Many, such as cucumbers and corn, require cross-pollination to produce viable seeds.

Do peas need nitrogen fertilizer to grow well?

Lois ❖ No. Peas require no supplemental nitrogen fertilizer, provided that they have treated with inoculant. Inoculant, which contains nitrogen-fixing bacteria, can be purchased with pea seed and dusted on the seeds before planting. Be sure to check the expiration date on the inoculant package.

Jim ❖ Nitrogen-fixing bacteria such as *Rhizobia* infect the roots of legumes, including peas. They allow the roots to extract nitrogen directly from the tiny pockets of air in the soil. Our atmosphere is 80 percent nitrogen, but many plants have no way to take advantage of it without nitrogen-fixing bacteria.

Should I soak my pea seeds prior to planting?

Lois ❖ No! There's no advantage in doing this. In fact, it often causes the peas to rot in the soil. Another problem that can arise is that fully saturated seeds placed in a dry garden have no additional source of moisture and can dry up and die. Just plant peas early into moist soil.

Jim ❖ Soaking pea seeds in water is never a good idea. As important as water is for germination, oxygen is equally important. Soaking seeds deprives them of oxygen and can literally drown them.

Last year I didn't get very good peas. What variety would you recommend?

Lois ❖ I like the traditional variety 'Lincoln' and the newer variety 'Eclipse' because they have excellent flavour and produce lots of peas. However, choosing the right variety is only one factor in succeeding with peas. You also have to plant early, so that the peas will mature before the summer heat sets in. I plant my peas as soon as the ground can be worked, since they love the cool weather and are very frost tolerant.

Jim ❖ Peas are prone to a variety of root-rot diseases that can cause the plants to suddenly turn brown. If your peas develop root rot, move the pea patch to another spot in the garden. No chemical controls exist for these diseases.

Peanuts

Can we grow peanuts in Canada? Are they sold as plants here?

Lois ❖ Peanuts are most closely associated with the southern United States, since they require warm temperatures and a long season to mature. I've grown short-season varieties for several years as a novelty plant here in Alberta. The yields aren't high and the nuts are small, but I manage to harvest a few tasty peanuts each year.

Jim ❖ Peanuts, like peas, are legumes and therefore enrich the soil with nitrogen. I find peanuts particularly interesting because the nuts don't grow on the roots. Instead, they're produced from the flowers. Once the bright-yellow flowers are pollinated, stems (peduncles) bend to the ground and pegs form at the flower's base. From these pegs, peanuts are produced.

Full sun and sandy soils are best for peanuts. If you live in a region with a short growing season, use only large peanut transplants of short-season varieties to ensure a crop before fall frost.

How do you know when peanuts are ready for harvest?

Jim ❖ Peanuts are a very long-season crop, so it's best to harvest them just after the first light fall frost. If you harvest early, the peanuts will be very small.

Peppers

Why do my peppers develop brown spots on the end of the fruit?

Lois ❖ I can't say for certain that this works, but I always mix eggshells around the base of my peppers. The shells contain calcium, and calcium is essential for preventing blossom end rot.

Jim ❖ Brown spots usually have one of two causes. Blossom end rot is caused by irregular water supply, coupled with a shortage of calcium in the soil. Brown blotches can also develop when the fruit has been suddenly exposed to lots of sunlight. Maintain lots of foliage protection for the fruit, and water and fertilize regularly.

What are the best temperatures for peppers?

Jim ❖ Peppers are native to tropical regions, so they love heat. Give them the hottest, sunniest spot in your garden. They need at least five hours of direct sunlight per day, but the more light, the better. Temperatures of 25–30°C are ideal, but even a few weeks of consistent temperatures in the low 20s will provide a good crop before the fall frost. When nighttime temperatures fall below about 10°C at night, fruit set is reduced. On the other hand, temperatures above 32°C can cause pollen sterility.

What is the difference between green and red peppers?

Lois ❖ Green peppers are simply less-ripe peppers. Red peppers have fully ripened.

What are the hottest pepper varieties? How is this measured?

Lois ❖ The top contenders are the scotch bonnet pepper and its close relative the habanero pepper. Both are hot enough that you should only handle them with rubber gloves. Scotch bonnet peppers are an essential ingredient in many Caribbean dishes.

Jim ❖ A pepper's heat comes from a chemical called capsaicin. The higher the concentration of capsaicin, the more potent the pepper. Scientists (and culinary masochists!) rate peppers according to the Scoville scale, a method for measuring capsaicin content.

Can we grow Hungarian hot peppers in Canada?

Lois ❖ Yes, you can grow Hungarian hot peppers. Just keep in mind that peppers require a long, warm growing season to produce good yields. Always start with robust, large transplants to get a jump start on the season.

Jim ❖ Hungarian isn't a true pepper category. However, a number of varieties within the salsa, hot, hybrid hot, sweet, and banana pepper types have the Hungarian designation tacked on. The term "Hungarian pepper" is similar to the term "Canadian bacon": it doesn't necessarily refer to the country of origin.

Do I need to cover peppers in case of frost?

Lois ❖ Peppers are very frost sensitive. Cover them with a good insulating fabric if there is even a slight risk of frost.

Jim ❖ Peppers can be left covered every night that the weather is cool. This will help to hold in heat and speed development. Just be sure to remove the cover during the day.

My green pepper plants were damaged by hail. The leaves are bent and some have holes in them, but otherwise the plant looks fine. Will they produce peppers?

Jim ❖ They should, provided that they weren't damaged too severely. Bent leaves usually recover quickly, and most small holes will heal over time. Severely hail-damaged pepper plants seldom recover sufficiently to produce a decent crop.

How do I know when I can pick my peppers?

Lois ❖ I know one commercial pepper-grower who recoils in horror at the thought of people harvesting and eating green peppers, mainly because green peppers are unripe. If you like green peppers, harvest them when they reach a mature size; otherwise, wait until they develop their full mature colour. Of course, in short-season areas, fall frost usually dictates when to harvest your peppers.

Are the peppers on my ornamental pepper plant edible?

Jim ❖ No, ornamental peppers are not edible. They are grown for their colourful, attractive fruit, but the plant contains an alkaloid called solanocapsine that is poisonous. Although it is unlikely to be lethal because absorption of the toxin through the digestive tract is small, I would not take the chance.

Popcorn

How do I know when my popcorn is ready to be harvested?

Lois ❖ Leave the ears on the plants until they are fully ripe. The kernels should contain sturdy, dry material, not a milky solution. Once they have reached maturity, pick the ears before they get soaked by heavy fall rains. Light showers or even a light frost won't hurt the cobs.

However, the kernels aren't ready for popping right after harvest. Popcorn must be properly dried or it will mould. After harvesting, remove the husks and spread the ears on boards or shelves in a cool, dry area out of the sun. You need just enough heat to keep the temperature above freezing. Popcorn cures slowly and will take about a month before it's thoroughly dried.

After the first month, you can try popping a few kernels each week. If all or most of the sample pops, remove all the kernels from the cob and store them in an air-tight plastic container. Wear gloves when you remove the dried kernels to avoid scratching your hands. Grasp the cob with two hands and twist.

Jim ❖ Popcorn is a very long-season crop. Never harvest it until the end of the season, when the kernels are very hard. The tassels should be brown and dry.

Potatoes

Which potato variety is the earliest?

Lois ❖ 'Warba' is still one of the earliest potato varieties. It has lovely white flesh and matures a couple of weeks earlier than many common potato varieties. However, they are not particularly good for baking and don't store well. They also have rather deep-set eyes that tend to trap soil, making them difficult to clean. I find them particularly tasty when they are small, so I always plant a few hills of 'Warba' specifically for early "baby" potatoes. I always have new potatoes by July, and occasionally I even have a few in late June!

My Yukon Gold potatoes look healthy when I harvest them. Why do they turn to mush when I boil them?

Lois ❖ This condition is known as sloughing and is a common problem with certain varieties grown under cool, wet conditions. Hope for better weather next year! In the meantime, try baking or steaming them.

The tops of my potato plants have turned brown. Can I harvest and store them now?

Lois ❖ Leave the tubers in the ground until about two weeks after the tops have browned or frosted down. This gives the skins time to set (toughen up) so that they can survive the rigours of storage.

Of course, if you're harvesting potatoes to eat right away, you can begin as soon as the tubers reach an acceptable size. What would summer be without new potatoes?

How do I know when I can begin harvesting potatoes to eat?

Lois ❖ A general guideline for determining when the tubers are beginning to form in the ground is when the potato plant flowers (although some varieties don't flower). I usually pull a few plants for early new potatoes when the plants are in full flower. If you are still unsure, you can also carefully tunnel into the soil from the side to see whether tubers have begun to develop.

Why do my new potatoes taste bitter?

Jim ❖ If your potatoes are green or bitter, don't eat them. Potatoes may taste bitter because they contain alkaloids called solanins. Solanins are poisonous if consumed in large quantities. Potatoes produce them to deter insect and animal feeding.

Tubers exposed to sunlight or even incandescent lights in storage can turn green and develop higher level of solanins. Bruised tubers can also contain high levels of solanins.

Will my potatoes freeze in the ground?

Lois ❖ A light frost will kill potato tops, but the tubers will be protected, provided they're completely covered by soil. However, potato tubers will be damaged by heavy frosts or prolonged temperatures below freezing.

Jim ❖ Although the potato tubers are protected against light frosts, don't leave them in the ground for long after the tops have been killed: a deep freeze will ruin the potatoes and they will be unusable.

How do I get rid of scab on potatoes?

Jim ❖ Scab disease causes scabby patches about 1 cm wide on the potato skins. The disease organism is very persistent in the soil, so rotating potatoes out of a spot for a year or two does little good. Consistent soil moisture, particularly after tubers set, reduces the incidence of scab. Avoid fresh manures, because they may carry the disease. And never plant scabby tubers or you will introduce the disease into your garden.

Fortunately, scab has little effect on the flesh beneath the skin. You can still peel the potatoes and eat them.

My potato plants are 3 feet tall. Should I cut them back?

Lois ❖ No. If you remove the tops, you'll remove the food-producing leaves that are essential for tuber growth.

Jim ❖ Excessively tall potato tops are usually a sign that you've applied too much compost, manure, or high-nitrogen fertilizer. As a result, you'll end up with more foliage and lower yields. This mistake can have a similar effect on tomatoes. Don't go overboard on nitrogen-rich fertilizer, unless your goal is to grow a lot of leaves!

If your potato plants are too tall, however, don't cut them back. You'll only make a bad situation worse.

What are the little things that look like tomatoes on top of my potato plant?

Lois ❖ These are the fruit of the potato plant. We often become so focussed on tuber production that we forget that potatoes produce flowers and fruit, just like tomato plants. In fact, potatoes and tomatoes are in the same family, Solanaceae.

Jim ❖ Even though potato fruit look similar to tomato fruit, don't be tempted to eat it. It contains high levels of toxic alkaloids, and eating it can make you extremely sick. Potatoes are related not only to tomatoes but also to deadly nightshade!

What are the little black dots just under the skin of my potatoes?

Jim ❖ There could be a few explanations, but the most likely cause is tuber flea beetles. These tiny black beetles (15–20 mm long) feed on the leaves first, leaving tiny "shot holes" in the foliage in early June to mid July. The larvae of the beetle tunnel into the potato tubers, leaving small brown or black streaks in the flesh. Tuber flea beetles were unheard of in my part of the world until about 15 years ago, when they found their way into Alberta. Now they are a regular pest of home-grown potatoes.

If you had tuber flea beetles, don't despair. The potatoes are still edible; just peel them deeper.

How do I control Colorado potato beetles?

Lois ❖ When I was a child back in Saskatchewan, we would knock them into buckets and drown them. It was effective, but rather gruesome! You can remove them by hand if the infestation is small. Several pesticides, if applied early, will eliminate the beetles before they can cause damage.

Jim ❖ Colorado potato beetles overwinter deep in the garden soil or in sheltered areas around the garden. Once the weather warms, the adult beetles seek out potato plants, feed, and lay clusters of bright-orange eggs on the undersides of the leaves.

Apply either Carbaryl (chemical insecticide) or Rotenone (organic insecticide) to the potato canopy. Or, if you're really determined and have a lot of time available, you can carefully check your plants, remove the leaves with eggs on them, and destroy the beetles before they even hatch.

My potatoes never flowered. Are they okay?

Lois ❖ Yes. Potatoes can form tubers without flowering.

What is this "Potato-Tomato" plant that I see advertised in some mail-order catalogues?

Jim ❖ The potato-tomato produces tomato fruits above ground, and potato tubers below. The plant is created by grafting a tomato shoot onto a potato stem. The tomato shoot base is cut into a wedge shape, inserted into the split stem of the potato, and then tied securely. One couple I know grafts an 'Early Girl' tomato onto a 'Norland' potato with good results. According to them, the tomatoes and potatoes taste better.

Some people speculate that toxins in the potato could move into the fruit, but to date this concern seems unfounded.

Pumpkins

How do I get green pumpkins to turn orange?

Lois ❖ If the pumpkins were harvested young and you can easily pierce the skin with your fingernail, they will not turn orange no matter what you do. However, if they have matured, you can sometimes cure green pumpkins by placing them in a bright, sunny, warm spot for a few weeks. (This is not a guaranteed solution, however.) Mature pumpkins can take a degree or two of frost but will be injured by lower temperatures.

Jim ❖ The concentration of carotenoids (yellow and orange compounds) will increase only slightly in storage, so your best is to harvest only fully coloured pumpkins.

How do I prevent pumpkins and squash from rotting off where they sit on the soil?

Lois ❖ Put dry mulch under the fruit. Use straw or other material that won't get soggy. Replace the mulch as it decomposes.

Jim ❖ Many disease organisms reside in the soil, and the moist space beneath the fruit provides an ideal environment for them. As Mom says, use mulch wherever possible.

Will my pumpkins continue to grow in the cool weather or should I bring them in now?

Lois ❖ Pumpkins effectively stop growing once temperatures are below 13°C during the day. You're best off harvesting them.

Jim ❖ Pumpkins can be injured by exposure to temperatures of 1–5°C for several days. The first sign is a "pitting" (tiny decaying spots) of the stem. Pitted pumpkins quickly rot in storage.

If I want to grow big pumpkins, should I prune them?

Lois ❖ Yes. If your objective is to grow a record-breaking pumpkin, then pruning is essential. Allow only one pumpkin per plant if you want to produce very large fruit.

Jim ❖ The leaves produce starches, sugars, and proteins—the building blocks for the pumpkin fruit. If you prune out all of the pumpkins except for one, all of those resources will go into that one, single fruit.

What variety of pumpkin produces the biggest fruit?

Jim ❖ Atlantic Giant is the largest "pumpkin" producer. It holds the world record at over 450 kg. And it's not just the fruits that are large: a single vine was once measured at over 42 m. Technically, however, Atlantic Giants aren't pumpkins—they're squash.

Radishes

Why do radishes go to seed?

Jim ❖ Radishes grow best under cool, moist conditions. When the days become long and warm, they respond by producing seed stalks, a process called bolting. I like to plant just a few radishes very early in the season and then plant again every couple of weeks beginning in late June through early August. The shorter days of late summer and early fall seem to alleviate this problem.

I've heard that I should plant radishes every week. Is this true?

Lois ❖ Yes. If you want a steady supply of radishes, you should plant a few every other week. Radishes grow quickly and become woody (go to seed and get tough) during periods of heat, drought, and long days.

Some commercial growers plant radishes as soon as they can work the soil in the spring, and then every week thereafter until August.

Is it true that I can mix radish and carrot seed together?

Lois ❖ Yes. Many gardeners use this trick. Radishes germinate and emerge very quickly and don't have trouble breaking through hard soil crusts. Carrots, on the other hand, germinate and emerge much more slowly, and often have difficulty with soil crusts. By mixing the two seeds together, you can enjoy an early harvest of radishes and leave behind nice, loose soil for the carrots, which mature later. In effect, you get two crops from a single row, so you're making excellent use of your garden space.

Spinach

How do I store spinach?

Lois ❖ Spinach is best planted often, and harvested regularly and quickly: it simply doesn't keep well!

Jim ❖ Fresh spinach doesn't store well, so you should eat it within a few days of harvest. Stored under ideal conditions—near the freezing point and at 95–100 percent relative humidity—it may last as long as 14 days. Of course, you're not likely to find these ideal conditions at your house.

How nutritious is spinach?

Jim ❖ Spinach is very high in vitamin A and is also a good source of vitamins C and B6. However, it also contains oxalic acid, which can impede the body's absorption of calcium.

Squash

Is squash suitable for a small garden?

Lois ❖ Squash will quickly outgrow any small garden. It is one of the largest and quickest-growing vegetables, with sprawling vines that spread out to fill all available space.

Jim ❖ The Atlantic Giant pumpkin, which is in fact a squash, has produced fruit weighing over 450 kg and vines of over 42 m in length. You're unlikely to have plants and fruit this big in your garden, but even an average squash plant can overtake a small plot. Fortunately, thanks to plant breeding, new bush varieties like 'Vegetable Marrow Bush' and 'Early Butternut' stay relatively compact.

How do I know when to pick my squash?

Lois ❖ Once the stem is hard and the fruit has darkened, the squash is ready for storage. Always make sure that you leave the stem attached to the fruit when you pick squash. If the stem break off, insects and disease can enter the wound and cause problems. It also shortens the storage life of the squash.

Jim ❖ If the squash is ripe enough to pick, you should be unable to break the skin easily with your fingernail.

Sweet potatoes

When do I harvest my sweet potatoes?

Lois ❖ Sweet potatoes are a long-season crop, so leave them in the ground until late in the season. Harvest shortly after the first light frost and store them in the house. By the way, did you know you can also eat the leaves of the sweet potato? That's right: they can be boiled or steamed like spinach!

Jim ❖ Never eat sweet potatoes right after harvest: they are watery and lack flavour. Their best flavour comes out only after many days of curing at warm temperatures. Ideally, they should be held at about 30°C for a week at high humidity—so put them in the warmest room in your home!

Tomatoes

I've picked my tomatoes and put them in a box. Now they're rotting. What should I do?

Lois ❖ Firm, ripe tomatoes don't last long in storage. Even under ideal conditions—7–10°C and very high humidity—they store poorly and will last less than a week. Mature green tomatoes last longer, for 3–4 weeks at 13–15° C and high humidity. Leaving the green stem attached to the fruit will help extend storage life.

Why are my tomato flowers falling off?

Lois ❖ Don't worry about "knocking off" flowers when you water your plants. You can't knock off good flowers but only weak flowers that were destined to fall anyway.

Jim ❖ It's normal for flowers to fall off after pollination, when they begin to set fruit. If they fall off sooner than that, it's usually due to stress. For tomatoes, that means excessively cool or hot weather, very dry conditions, or low light levels.

Why do my tomato plants wilt in the heat of the day?

Jim ❖ Several factors can cause tomatoes to wilt on hot days:

- Newly transplanted tomatoes have a smaller root system and simply can't absorb enough water.
- The plants are growing in dry soil.
- If the weather is exceptionally hot, the tomatoes may give up moisture through their foliage faster than they can absorb water through their roots.
- Injury to roots and stems from disease or insects can interfere with water absorption.

The bottom of my tomato fruit turns black. Why?

Lois ❖ This condition is known as blossom end rot. It occurs if the tomato plant dries out while the fruit is growing.

Keep the soil consistently moist. This is particularly important for containerized tomatoes, because the soil moisture levels can fluctuate so quickly. Always use large containers for tomatoes, because they hold more moisture.

Jim ❖ Blossom end rot is actually caused by calcium deficiency. Unless the root zone is kept consistently moist, the plant can't absorb enough calcium from the soil. Calcium keeps cell walls solid. Without it, the fruit cells literally fall apart and leak, causing the blossom end of the tomato to shrivel and turn black.

One of my tomato plants has bumps along the lower part of the stem. What is it, and will it infect my other plants?

Jim ❖ Those bumps aren't a disease. They're dormant or adventitious roots—that is, roots that develop along the stem. If this portion of the stem is exposed to moist soil, those bumps will develop into roots. Some tomato growers take advantage of this fact by transplanting their tomatoes deeper to encourage more root production.

It's mid August. Why haven't my tomatoes fruited yet?

Jim ❖ Tomato plants that haven't fruited by August won't produce mature fruit before frost. There could be several reasons for your problem.

• You may have transplanted too late.

• The tomato plants may have received insufficient sunlight.

• Too much compost (an excess of nitrogen) may have reduced blooming because of excessive leaf production.

• You may have pruned improperly.

• Cool weather may have diminished flowering.

• Disease may have destroyed your flowers.

• In a short-season growing area, you may be growing varieties that are unsuitable for the gardening season (i.e., late-maturing varieties).

What is the best pot size for container-grown tomatoes?

Lois ❖ I won't plant tomatoes in any container smaller than 15 litres. If the container is too small, the plants won't get enough moisture and nutrients to develop properly.

Jim ❖ As a general rule at our greenhouse, we use 20-litre plastic buckets for growing tomatoes. They don't fall over and the roots have plenty of room to grow. I like to leave a 5–8 cm lip above the soil level. Each time I water and fertilize, I fill the container to the top and let the excess drain through. This ensures the plant receives adequate moisture and nutrients.

Why are my tomato leaves curling?

Lois ❖ Two things can cause this. If the new growth is excessively twisted or distorted, the plants may have been exposed to 2,4-D or similar volatile weed-killers. If all of the leaves are curling, chances are the soil has been too dry. Give the roots a good, thorough soaking, and the plants will likely not suffer any serious long-term damage.

Jim ❖ Tomatoes have the potential for curling locked in their genes. It is a recessive trait, while flat leaves are the dominant trait. Curling can appear naturally and is no cause for alarm if weed-killer or water are not the problem.

Fall frost is approaching and my tomatoes are all green. How can I ripen them?

Lois ❖ Small, hard green tomatoes will never mature once they're picked. More mature tomatoes will continue to ripen after harvest.

Here's one excellent technique. If the tomatoes are still green, but almost ready to ripen, pull the entire plant out of the ground with the fruit still attached. Shake off the soil, and hang the plant in the garage. The fruit will ripen better and last longer than it would if you removed it from the vine.

When should I prune my tomato plant? How should I prune it?

Jim ❖ It depends whether the tomato is determinate or indeterminate. Determinate tomatoes form bushes and do not need to be pruned. Indeterminate tomatoes, also called staking tomatoes, grow very tall and should be pruned.

When pruning, remove the axillary shoots (suckers) all the way up the stem while they are still small. You'll spot these tiny new shoots sprouting at the points where the side branches meet the stem. Simply pinch them out. Be careful not to remove flower clusters.

What does "VFN" mean on tomato seed packages?

Jim ❖ This acronym means that the variety is resistant to three serious pests: verticillium (V), fusarium (F), and nematodes (N).

- Verticillium: a fungal disease that resides in soil and infects plants, causing wilt.
- Fusarium: a fungal disease that attacks roots and crowns.
- Nematodes: very tiny, worm-like pests that attack roots.

These pests pose more of a threat in some regions than in others. A VFN tomato will be more pest resistant, but no variety is completely immune.

Explain trenching tomatoes.

Lois ❖ Trenching is a method of planting tomatoes. It involves laying the roots, crown, and a portion of the stem in the soil to encourage better rooting.

Tomatoes have the ability to produce adventitious roots from the stem. In other words, new roots will sprout all the way up the stem after being in moist soil for a week or two.

Jim ❖ I have not noticed superior yield from trenching tomatoes, although it does help to anchor the plant against strong winds. Trench-planting is often done when a tomato seedling has stretched and could benefit from a better base in the soil; such a plant will not suffer from losing a portion of its stem.

Do tomatoes need bees for pollination?

Jim ❖ No. Tomatoes are almost entirely self-pollinated. Each flower produces pollen that fertilizes its own stigma and produces a fruit. Wind encourages pollen shed and thus aids pollination.

Many commercial greenhouses do use bumblebees or mechanical methods to assist pollination, however, because there is insufficient air movement in that environment.

The leaves of my tomato plant are crisp and dry on the ends. Why?

Lois ❖ Crisp leaves are usually caused by drought. This can be a particular problem with tomatoes grown in pots, because they tend to dry out so quickly. An overdose of fertilizer can also turn the leaf edges brown. This condition is what people mean when they talk about "burning" a plant with fertilizer.

Jim ❖ Tomatoes have higher salt tolerance than many plants, so burning is not a common problem, but it's still important to water regularly and not to over-fertilize.

Why are the leaves of my tomato plant yellow and drooping?

Jim ❖ Any disease that attacks the roots or stem can lead to wilting. Your plant may have a soil-borne disease called Verticillium Wilt. This disease destroys the stem tissues, causing the plants to turn yellow and wilt. Remove infected plants and don't plant tomatoes in that location for the next few years.

Should I prune my tomato down to the base to make it bush out more?

Lois ❖ No! You'll severely injure the plant if you strip off the leaves.

Jim ❖ Severe pruning removes leaves that produce the sugars for fruit production. Prune only the axillary vegetative shoots.

How tall can a tomato plant grow?

Jim ❖ If the growing season were long enough, an indeterminate tomato plant could reach 9 metres or better. Greenhouse tomatoes commonly grow 3–5 metres tall. Indeterminate garden varieties tend to average 1–1.5 metres.

How much fruit does a 'Tumbler' tomato produce?

Jim ❖ Many people have had over 300 tomatoes on a single 'Tumbler' plant. However, the plant often doesn't have enough energy to produce so many fruit at once. The fruit's demand for sugars will outstrip the plant's ability to assimilate them.

I prefer to let only a couple of dozen fruit set at one time. This involves pruning out extra flower clusters. You may hate to do this, but it's worth it. If you don't want to do this, be sure you grow the plant in a large pot (at least 20 L), water regularly, and fertilize at least once a week to give the plant enough nutrients to support all that fruit.

Do you need to stake 'Tumbler' tomatoes?

Lois ❖ No. 'Tumbler' is a bush tomato and does not require stalking.

How big a basket do I need for my 'Tumbler'?

Lois ❖ Don't use anything smaller than a 30-cm hanging basket. You may find it easier to grow in a 40-cm basket. Bigger baskets are better.

How long until my 'Tumbler' tomato starts to trail?

Lois ❖ 'Tumbler' tomatoes grow very quickly under the right conditions. Two months after you plant the seed, a 'Tumbler' may be trailing over the edge of a 30-cm hanging basket.

Should the water drain out of my 'Tumbler' tomato hanging basket when I water it?

Jim ❖ Yes! A 'Tumbler' consumes a tremendous amount of water and fertilizer. Don't stop watering until the water begins running from the bottom. Be sure, though, that the water is soaking into the soil and not simply running down between the soil and the side of the pot. If the soil in your basket has dried to the point that the soil has shrunk from the sides, put the entire basket in a container of water until the rootball is completely saturated.

Can I plant a 'Tumbler' tomato in the garden?

Lois ❖ The 'Tumbler' has a prostrate growth habit, which means that it grows close to the ground. If you grow a 'Tumbler' in the garden, much of the fruit will rest on the soil and rot. They perform best in raised containers and hanging baskets.

How many tomatoes will I get from one plant? Will I get as many tomatoes this year as last?

Jim ❖ In general, you can expect about 4–5 kg per plant for large transplants grown in a good environment. However, yield depends on several factors:

• The larger and more mature the transplant, the larger the potential yield.

• Some varieties produce greater yields than others.

• The longer the growing season (providing the season is warm and sunny), the greater the yield.

• Adequate fertilizer, water, sunlight, and good soil greatly enhance yield.

If I plant my tomato plants in June, will I still get tomatoes this year?

Lois ❖ Yes, if the transplants are large. You should also shop for earlier varieties.

Jim ❖ A small seedling planted in June will not likely produce mature fruit before the first fall frost except in warm regions with a very long season.

My recently transplanted tomatoes are turning yellow. What's wrong?

Jim ❖ They might not be getting enough water or fertilizer. Very cool weather can also cause new transplants to turn yellow.

The lowest leaves on my tomato plant are turning yellow, but the rest of the plant seems fine. What should I do?

Lois ❖ If the plants are getting plenty of water, try increasing the fertilizer rates. Yellow lower leaves on otherwise healthy, well-watered plants usually indicate a shortage of nitrogen.

Jim ❖ If only the lower leaves are turning yellow, it's likely a lack of nitrogen. Yellowing can also be due to a fungal infection or root rot.

I have tomato plants with blight. If I pull them out, can I replant new ones in the same soil?

Jim ❖ Blight is a generic term for disease. Some tomato diseases reside and persist in the soil, and others do not. Unless you can positively identify the disease, there's no way to know whether it's safe to replant tomatoes in that location.

If you've had a persistent problem year after year, give the area a rest and either plant tomatoes in a container in pasteurized potting soil or put them in an entirely new spot in the garden.

Is there a tomato that will grow well on an east-facing balcony?

Jim ❖ I'm afraid you're out of luck. Tomatoes need a minimum of five hours of direct afternoon sunlight for reasonable growth. If the area is too dark, few fruit will form and those that do will not taste as good as those grown in full sun. Low light levels prevent the proper development of the flavour-enhancing compounds in the fruit.

What tomato variety produces the biggest fruit?

Lois ❖ The variety 'Delicious' holds the world record for the largest tomato ever grown (3.5 kg). Other varieties that produce very large fruit are 'Beefmaster' (up to 1 kg) and 'Brandywine' (500–700 g).

Jim ❖ But if you're interested in prolific production, 'Sungold' holds the record, producing more than 1,000 tomatoes on a single plant.

Are there special tomatoes for making paste?

Lois ❖ Yes. Paste tomatoes are bred for their high solids content. In other words, they are less watery than most tomatoes. This makes them excellent for sauces and salads. 'Laroma' is my favourite paste variety.

What variety of tomatoes should I grow in my greenhouse?

Lois ❖ Many tomatoes grow well in the greenhouse, so it's really a matter of personal choice. My personal favourites are 'Big Beef,' 'Counter,' 'Sun Sugar,' and 'Vendor.'

What is the best tomato for beginner gardeners?

Lois ❖ Your best bet is to start with a large transplant. That way, you avoid all of the problems that can occur early in the plant's life cycle. Bush tomatoes are simpler to grow than indeterminate tomatoes, because they don't require pruning or staking. Choose earlier-maturing varieties, such as 'Early Girl' and 'Sugar Snack' so that if your conditions are less than optimum, you still have a chance of success.

Most tomato seed packets and seedlings are labelled with the "days to maturity." Does this refer to the time from seeding, transplanting, or blossom set?

Jim ❖ The rating refers to the estimated number of days between transplanting a reasonably sized seedling and harvesting the fruit. However, the actual time this takes depends a lot on the weather. Tomatoes prefer daytime temperatures in the mid 20s and nights in the mid to upper 10s. A stretch of cool weather will add to the number of days it takes for tomatoes to mature.

Use the "days to maturity" rating only as a guide to compare one variety to the next. It's an estimate, not an absolute.

Should I cut the tops off my indeterminate tomatoes to speed the ripening of the fruit?

Lois ❖ Don't remove the top until a few weeks before fall frost. Depending on your region, you should begin in August or early September.

When you cut off the top, you stop the plant from putting energy into new growth, shifting it into the fruit instead. Late in the season, tiny tomatoes don't have enough time to mature before frost, so prune them off as well.

What is the earliest tomato variety we have?

Lois ❖ That's a tough race to call, since much depends upon location, climate, and so many other factors. However, I will say that Early Girl is consistently one of the earliest-maturing varieties.

My tomato plants are up 6 inches. Can I fertilize them yet?

Jim ❖ There's no reason to wait even that long. Begin feeding your tomatoes early and often. They're heavy feeders. I use 10-52-10 once a week for 3 weeks after transplanting. After that, I use 20-20-20 or 15-15-30 once a week.

Which fertilizer should I use on my tomatoes? Are spikes better than ready-mixes?

Lois ❖ I like spikes if I'm in a rush. They're easy to use and almost foolproof.

Jim ❖ There is no one best fertilizer, but water-soluble fertilizers like 15-15-30 and 20-20-20 are excellent. Fertilizer spikes work quite well, but water-soluble fertilizers can be absorbed by the roots much more quickly.

Do yellow tomatoes taste the same as red tomatoes?

Lois ❖ Flavour can differ by variety, soil types, and weather conditions. Yellow tomatoes tend to have a milder flavour than red tomatoes. But this does not mean that yellow varieties don't taste every bit as good as red ones—one bite of 'Sun Sugar' will quell that notion!

Turnips

What's the difference between turnips and rutabagas?

Lois ❖ Turnips are often referred to as summer turnips. They have mild-tasting, off-white flesh and are often smaller than rutabagas. Rutabagas have stronger-tasting, yellow flesh and, unlike turnips, can be kept for months in cold storage. Personally, I love them both!

Jim ❖ Turnips leaves are usually lighter green, hairy, and quite thin, while rutabaga leaves are thick, smooth, and bluish green.

Watermelon

How do I know if my watermelons are ripe?

Lois ❖ Rap your watermelon sharply with your knuckles. You should hear a dull thud when the watermelon is ripe. This is also a handy trick to use in the grocery store!

Zucchini

Why are my zucchini black on the ends?

Jim ❖ Like tomatoes, zucchini can suffer from blossom end rot. Fortunately, the remedy is the same, too—just make sure to water consistently and remove any fruit that exhibits symptoms of blossom end rot to ensure that the plant puts energy only into healthy fruit.

I've grown too much zucchini. Would you like to have some of it?

Lois ❖ No, thanks—I've got plenty of my own!

Afterword

by Jim Hole

I love to learn. I guess that's why I've always been more interested in the mechanics of the real world than the imaginary narratives of novels or films. Don't get me wrong—I love a good story as much as the next guy, but a chance to learn about the inner workings of nature holds more appeal for me. Sometimes Mom describes me as a kind of walking gardening encyclopaedia, but the truth is, as you might have guessed, a little more complex. Although my sister-in-law calls me "Mr. Science," I don't pretend to know everything. But it bugs me if someone asks me a question and I don't know the answer. More often than not, the solution isn't in my head; I have to pull out a textbook or consult a specialist. Over the years I've naturally assimilated plenty of gardening knowledge because of that inability to let a question go without a response. Putting together these books has been very fulfilling for that reason; your questions gave me plenty of opportunity to do some extra research, and to discover a number of things I wasn't previously aware of.

So what's my favourite vegetable? I'd have to say corn, for both its fantastic sweet flavour and the challenge of growing a good stand in a fairly short-season climate. Growing corn in northern Alberta is kind of like an exciting horse race. Just as you can often tell who the winner is going to be after the first leg of the race, if the corn stalks aren't "thigh-high by the first of July," you know it's going to be a tight contest between the corn reaching maturity and the onset of fall frost. And a heavy yield of sweet, tender cobs is, to me, the best prize in gardening.

So Ask Us Some Questions...

We plan to update all of the Question and Answer books periodically. If you have a gardening question that's been troubling you, write to us! While we can't answer your inquiries individually, your question may appear in future Q&A books–along with the answer, naturally. And don't ever think that a question is "dumb" or "too simple." Odds are that any mysteries you face are shared by countless other gardeners.

Send your questions to:

Hole's Q&A Questions
101 Bellerose Drive
St. Albert, AB T8N 8N8
CANADA

You can also send us e-mail at yourquestions@enjoygardening.com, or visit us at www.enjoygardening.com.

Index

Question: *Who is Lois Hole?*

Answer: the author of eight best-selling books, Lois Hole provides practical advice that's both accessible and essential. Her knowledge springs from years of hands-on experience as a gardener and greenhouse operator. She's shared that knowledge for years through her books, her popular newspaper columns, hundreds of gardening talks all over the continent, and dozens of radio and television appearances. Never afraid to get her hands dirty, Lois answers all of your gardening questions with warmth and wit.

A member of the Order of Canada, Lois is the recipient of honorary degrees from Athabasca University and the University of Alberta, where she served as Chancellor from 1998-2000. She currently serves as Alberta's Lieutenant Governor.

Question: *Who is Jim Hole?*

Answer: Inheriting his mother's love of horticulture, Jim Hole grew up in the garden. After spending his formative years on the Hole farm in St. Albert, Jim attended the University of Alberta, expanding his knowledge and earning a Bachelor of Science in Agriculture. Jim appears regularly on radio and television call-in shows to share what he's learned, and writes regular gardening columns for the *Edmonton Journal*, the *National Post*, the *Old Farmer's Almanac*, and the *Old Farmer's Almanac Gardener's Companion*. He has also contributed to *Canadian Gardening* magazine. Jim's focus is on the science behind the garden; he explains what makes plants tick in a clear and concise style, without losing sight of the beauty and wonder that makes gardening worthwhile.

Lois and Jim have worked together for years on books, newspaper articles, and gardening talks. With family members Ted Hole, Bill Hole, and Valerie Hole, Lois and Jim helped create Hole's, a greenhouse and garden centre that ranks among the largest retail gardening operations in Canada. The books in the Q&A series mark Lois and Jim's first official collaboration as authors.

One last question...

How was the Vegetables Q & A book made?

We've been growing vegetables for more than 40 years and they are still our favourite plants in the garden. So *Vegetables* was an obvious topic for a Q&A book. Our greenhouse and garden centre staff collected the initial questions. **Bill Hole** and **Bruce Keith** sorted through the questions, suggested a few more, and started drawing up a list of charts and sidebars. Then **Jim Hole** sat down to sketch the answers to the questions. This first round of answers was passed to **Lois** and **Ted Hole** for their perspective and input.

The manuscript was then given to **Scott Rollans**, the series editor, who transformed the raw material into book form. Jim went through Scott's reorganized text, checking facts and correcting errors. Meanwhile, **Earl Woods** collected extra material for the book and worked with the Hole family to create the chapter introductions. The now-near-final text was passed to **Leslie Vermeer** to check for consistency, clarity, and correctness. After this edit, the manuscript went back to **Valerie Hole** and the rest of the family to resolve any remaining queries. Concurrently, the text hit the production department, and designer **Greg Brown** and archivist **Christina McDonald** selected pictures for the book. Greg integrated the text, photographs, charts, and illustrations on the computer to produce electronic layouts. When all the pieces were in place, we all checked the text one last time.

The electronic files, along with the digital images, fonts, and associated graphics, were collected and burned to CD for transport to **Elite Lithographers**. Elite prepared the files using their Apogee pre-press system, and printed final digital proofs for the Hole's staff to check. With any last-minute changes indicated, the proofs were returned to Elite, who made the revisions and downloaded the processed files to their Agfa Avantra 44 imagesetter. The imagesetter produced nine large pieces of film, each representing sixteen pages of the final book. The film was shipped to **Quality Color Press**'s pre-press department, where the film was burned to the printing plates. These were mounted on a 40-inch Heidelberg SM press to be printed on 60-pound Husky offset paper. The sheets were printed 16 book pages to a side and then machine folded. The folded sheets were sent to **Bindery Overload** for final assembly. At the bindery, the folded sheets were collated with the colour covers, printed separately, and bound by a perfect binder. Then Lois and Jim's latest book was loaded into boxes for shipment to bookstores across the continent.

Publication Management ❖ Bruce Timothy Keith
Series Editor ❖ Scott Rollans
Editor ❖ Leslie Vermeer
Writing & Editing ❖ Earl J. Woods
Book Design and Production ❖ Gregory Brown